Industry 4.0
Data Analytics

Rajesh Agnihotri

and

Samuel New

Copyright © 2012 Rajesh Agnihotri, Samuel New

All rights reserved.

ISBN:1534778284
ISBN-13: 978-1534778283

DEDICATION

To those who admire change, may this book let you take what once was, and what is, and shape what will be.

CONTENTS

Chapter 1 A Glance At Industry 3.0   Page 2

Chapter 2 Push For Next Industrial Revolution Page 19

Chapter 3 Emergence Of Digital Supply Chain   Page 43

Chapter 4 Setting An Analytics Culture   Page 89

Chapter 5 Analysis 101   Page 122

Chapter 6 Inventory Management Data Analysis   Page 152

ACKNOWLEDGMENTS

We would like to thank our respective families for supporting us in our endeavor. Writing this book involved countless hours of planning, research, and editing, and it often meant sacrificing precious time with our families. However never once did they complain, and it is only because of their love and encouragement that this book came to fruition. We would also like to acknowledge our editor, Pranav Agnihotri, who spent hours upon hours reading and rereading our material, helping us shape our book into the finished product it finally is after nine months of hard work. And finally, we would like to thank you, the reader, for giving our book a chance and giving meaning to the work that we put into it by reading it and hopefully gaining valuable insight into our world. Without you, this book our work is meaningless.

CHAPTER ONE

A GLANCE AT INDUSTRY 3.0
"All Advantages are temporary"

Understanding Industry 3.0

Many of us have been intrigued by Nostradamus' enigmatic predictions. For those not familiar with the legendary figure, Nostradamus was a renowned prophet born on December 14, 1503 in France.

Nostradamus was believed to be ahead of his time and has been said to have had made numerous predictions about key events in world history, from the Great Fire of London, rise of Napoleon and Adolf Hitler, to the September 2001 attacks on the World Trade Center. Furthermore, besides predicting world events, Nostradamus is said to have predicted his own death. It is said that on July 1, 1566, when his assistant wished him goodnight, he gravely proclaimed, "You will not find me alive at sunrise."

He was found dead the next morning.

But whether or not his powers were real, or these accounts are all simply fabricated myths, it is undeniable that the concept of foreseeing the future is something that has fascinated and gripped even the least curious of minds for eons. Ever since we came into existence, humans have been trying to master the ability to forecast and divine the future, using both technology and the coveted sixth sense.

Who would deny the power of accurate prediction? Predicting and building the product that would be an instant hit with customers; predicting the perfect sales forecast for the next quarter, and building just enough quantity to avoid inventory shortages or surpluses; predicting and betting on the investment that would yield the maximum return, or exiting well in time prior to the market crash; predicting natural calamities and proactively taking appropriate actions, and of course, predicting the winning horse at a derby race. And especially in our current day and age, where globally both customers and businesses are tightly interlocked and there is a far greater need to make accurate and timely decisions, we all need an all seeing crystal ball of our own.

An example of this idea of gazing into the future and its benefits was admirably demonstrated by Amazon, the e-commerce giant. In a world that is witnessing a growing adoption of online shopping, Amazon has been a front runner in the field of taking innovative approaches in delivering this service. And in 2012, Amazon did something beyond remarkable in the realm of prediction and forecasting. They filed a patent for an algorithm that enabled Amazon to do anticipatory shipping.

The Algorithm known by the name "Method and system for anticipatory package shipping", describes a method for shipping a package of one or more items "to the destination geographical area without completely specifying the delivery address at time of shipment," with the final destination defined en route.

It's difficult to comprehend how Amazon is able to start delivering packages, when a customer has not even placed an online order yet. But through their copyrighted algorithm, they have managed to predict customer's orders with a very low error rate, and this has had a tremendous benefit in terms of increased sales, enhanced resource utilization, reduced shipping and reduced inventory and end to end supply chain cost.

Now, it is important to understand the motivation behind Amazon's drive to have this sort of capability in place. With globalization, market competition is already very intense, and with e-commerce, this battle for customers has soared to insane heights. Most businesses today are struggling to sustain their growth; pulling every trick from the hat to try and differentiate themselves from the sea of competitors that are also doing the same. So with it becoming more and more difficult to attract customers and pull them away from the other competitors, the common theme for online retailers has become to master the ability to stop customers from visiting physical stores, and try to provide them with great customer experience through ease of funneling through myriads of online products, and delivering physical products to them at the speed of light.

But the deciding factor for many online shoppers is the Products and Services delivery quality and speed. This can build or shatter a customer experience, and so is the most crucial factor that makes or breaks an online business. Amazon relies heavily on the predictive data modeling that takes in various streams of data, like customers order history, product search browsing history, removed items from online customer's shopping carts, customer mouse duration over an item, wish lists, product rating and many more similar factors. Through this algorithm, Amazon is able to up the level of customer product delivery experience and keep them coming back.

Similarly, physical retailers are doing their own share of innovation to keep the customers coming back. Having realized the developing inclination of tech savvy customers towards online shopping, many have adopted a hybrid model that provides customer with an additional option of online shopping through websites, and mobile application. In later chapters, we will share some of the processes that these brick and mortar retailers are adopting to stay ahead in the game, that make use of technology.

However, whatever companies do, industrial competition will always exist, and shall continue to inspire new innovations that from time to time, will result in radical new processes or technology that will disrupt the market and will effectively be game changers. The rate of technological advancements has picked up to a pace where this disruption cycle has drastically reduced, reinforcing the "change is the only constant" paradigm.

And with all these advancements that we have made in business models and in technology, we now stand at the juncture of the emergence of digital industrialization, commonly referred to as Industries 4.0. Cyber-Physical convergence is transforming our lives, how we behave as a customer, and how we conduct as a business entity. Internet of Things (IoT), Big Data, Drones, and 3-D Printing are just a few examples of new technologies that are causing disruptions in the market place, and are enabling us to reach territories which were never before accessible.

However, before we dwell deeper on the Digital Industrial Revolution, we believe it is important for you to appreciate, and understand the key events in the life cycle of the Industrial era that we are slowly leaving behind; the Industrial Era, commonly referred to as Industries 3.0.

Industries 3.0: Innovation Timeline

To be precise, we consider the time between 1970 and 2010 as demarcating the era of Industries 3.0. Since technological advancement heavily influenced the global industrial transformation, I think it is important to first start with presenting a few key technology events, followed by an analysis of how it enabled global markets to expand, and commerce to thrive.

PLC (Programmable Logic Controller)
The new era of manufacturing back then, was marked by the introduction of PLC (Programmable Logic Controller) by Dick Morley and his fellow "geeks", who sold the first PLC to General Motors.

Image Source: library.automationdirect.com

In today's era of incredibly ubiquitous fast computing, it is hard to appreciate and visualize the productivity, and operational improvement this invention triggered.

As part of my first job, I had the opportunity to work on some extremely old relay logic run machines that had huge electrical control panels similar to the picture shown above. There were numerous challenges associated with designing, building machine logic, and operating and troubleshooting these machines. However the biggest problem, was the lack of flexibility to make changes to the machine logic. A minor change would mean having to re-route cables and add or remove hardware components. On the other hand a major change would mean literally re-designing all aspects of the system.

Indeed, Manufacturing was changed forever with the introduction of PLC, and soon, this programmable logic controller became the de-facto way, to develop machine operating logic.

Image Source: RepairZone.com

This digital controller automated industrial electromechanical processes, and gave the end customers the ability to program and bring changes to the electromechanical system during its useful life, at a very low cost compared to the custom built controller design, which increased the ease and efficiency of operations.

Personal Computer & Mobile Communication

This era also witnessed the birth of the Personal Computer. The journey of the evolution of computers and the history of its origin with the military is a remarkable story, that although is not within the scope of this book, is something that I highly recommend you explore later on. Moving on, in April 1974, Intel introduced the 8080 microprocessor chip, and addressed 64kb of memory that was part of the Altair kit, that many considered the first personal computer. The kit was sold for $395, and had to be assembled after purchase; a much more difficult process than today's assemble-at-home products as this required a soldering iron to finish the circuit boards.

Then, on April 1st 1976, Steve Jobs and Stephen Wozniak founded their company Apple, and in 1977, launched Apple II at $1,298 as their first personal computer designed for the mass market. Priced at $1,565 IBM introduced its first personal computer M5100 in 1981, that had 16kb of memory, a built-in 16 lines by 64 character display, a built in DC-300 cartridge tape drive for storage, an Intel processor chip, and the MS DOS 1.0 (disk operating system) from a 32-person company called Microsoft.

On the data storage side, the 1970's witnessed the introduction of the 8" and 5.25" floppy disk; a portable, magnetic storage device which is read and written by a floppy disk drive. Floppy disks became the ubiquitous form of data storage and exchange from mid 70s well into 2000.

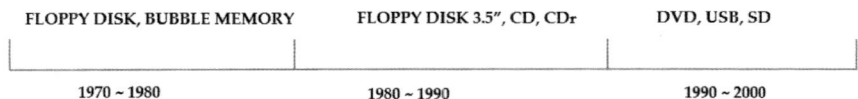

FLOPPY DISK, BUBBLE MEMORY	FLOPPY DISK 3.5", CD, CDr	DVD, USB, SD
1970 ~ 1980	1980 ~ 1990	1990 ~ 2000

In 1973, the first mobile phone call was made by Martin Cooper, an executive, and a researcher at Motorola, using a 2 pound prototype of the world's first portable cellular telephone using the DynaTAC (Dynamic Adaptive Total Area Coverage) system. This was a technological breakthrough and it opened so many new possibilities for the way of life of customers, and an avenue of income for companies that would spring up around this concept of mobile phones.

Networks data communications standards such as RS485, CAN and Ethernet

were developed. Hence, the industry ushered into the age of computers, electronics communication, and electronically controlled manufacturing.
Data Collection Technologies & ERP

One of the profound changes that these communication technologies caused was that now Data became an asset, and technology enabled it to move, store, and most importantly, be efficiently analyzed.

Throughout history, the science of collection, presentation, analysis and interpretation of numerical data that is statistics, has been used by governments for planning activities, the creation of censuses and much more. However before the invention of computers, the methods of collecting data were naturally very crude and inefficient by comparison.

To give you a perspective, the 1880 USA census took 7 years to process the collected census data, before arriving with a meaningful report. Later on in 1890, Herman Hollerith invented the "Tabulating Machine" (shown below) which had the ability to process data on punch cards. That reduced the 1890 census time to 18 months, and resulted in a smaller budget.

Image Source: Zdnet.com

Furthermore, advances in computer technology enabled advances in the data collection mechanisms. The real breakthrough came with the appearance of Relational Database, which was born in 1970 when E.F. Codd, a researcher from IBM wrote a paper, explaining the process that enabled a departure from flat file based databases.

First_Name	Last_Name	Age	City
Frank	Anthony	34	LA
James	Brown	42	CA
Mike	Page	29	ON
Jasmeet	Singh	44	BC

First_Name,Last_Name,Age,City|Frank, Anthony,34,LA|
James, Brown,42,CA|
Mike, Page, 29, ON|
Jasmeet,Singh,44, BC

Relational databases use the concept of tables to arrange data. The standard fields from each record are represented as column (fields), and rows (records) in a table. This made searching for stored information quicker and allowed users to write a simple data query to create tables, extract, and update information in a breeze using Sequel (SQL) language.

The advent of relational databases was the turning point for data analytics. With ease of setting, collecting, and managing data, it gained tremendous traction, and adoption within the industries that enabled users to push the boundaries of what they could now do with the data. Prior to the computerization of data, essentially every business transaction (internal and external) and record management was done manually. Integrating an external ecosystem of suppliers and customers within the business was not technologically feasible and so the notion existed only academically. But with the onset of new technology centered around data collection and computerization, businesses with access to the mass manufactured personal computers, started to capture and use more and more inter functional data for making business decisions. New graphical computer interfaces, and flexible excel spreadsheets, enabled huge improvements in business and operational planning and execution.

Black and Decker became the first company to implement MRP (master requirements planning), a production planning, scheduling, and inventory control system in their manufacturing process. They also used IBM mainframe computers to explode and decipher individual component information from BOM (bill of material) for finish products and used it in scheduling the purchasing and production of plans for components.

To take another example, Walmart, the famous American multinational retail corporation, first started the use of Information Technology in 1975. Walmart bought an IBM mainframe system to have better inventory control and management, and achieved that through creating a system of computerized inventory tracking in their distribution systems. Considered a cutting edge technology then, it gave Walmart unprecedented competitive advantage. In the early 1980's, Walmart adopted the barcode system, an optical machine-readable representation of data relating to the object to which it is attached, to scan the products, and let the rest be handled by the computer. Objects that previously needed to be rung by a knowledgeable cashier could now be quickly scanned. This drastically reduced the checkout time and made inventory tracking and capturing POS (point of sale) data a breeze.

But soon business environments started to grow too complex, with creation of pockets of silo databases, and applications within company functional units, that seldom talked to each other. Data and application redundancy started to creep in, and businesses started to realize the need for of a common cross-functional view of data flow for making holistic business decisions at various points in the supply chain, ranging from making efficient procurement buying decisions, inventory management, accounting, planning human resources requirements, logistic decisions around product, and services distribution. Introduced in the 1980's, ERP systems (Enterprise Resource Planning), which were essentially software systems for enterprise wide planning, encompassed various specialized modules for areas such as Material management (MM), Sales and distribution (SD), Production, Planning and Control (PPC), Quality Management (QM), Financial modules, and much more. This gained huge market traction by late 1990's. ERP Systems had the ability to create enterprise wide integration by utilizing one database, one application, and unified interface across the enterprise, thus improving both core and front-end functions.

The German company SAP AG (Systems, Applications and Products in Data Processing), was started in the early 70's by 5 ex-IBM engineers in Germany, who produced their first ERP SAP R/2 in 1979. This was an integrated business application targeting material management and production planning tasks within a manufacturing enterprise. SAP R/2 was using a mainframe utilizing centralized database that improved data maintenance. However SAP's biggest breakthrough came with the launch of SAP R/3 ERP in 1999 that had client/ server architecture.

Role of Information Technology in Globalization
In the mid 90's, the term "Supply Chain" gained widespread recognition as a result of the globalization of manufacturing industries. This was primarily a result of manufacturing companies who started outsourcing their internal functions which were not considered part of the core business activity and suddenly outsourcing found a place in boardrooms and became the new business strategy for competitive advantage.

Outsourcing created a paradigm shift, from being a vertically integrated company that grappled with creating competitive advantages through managing, and enhancing end to end functions using internal resources, to an agile and flexible company that focused on creating and enhancing strategies around their core business, and identified external partners to execute non-critical functions.

And although seemingly new to the table at the time, outsourcing wasn't an alien concept. It was quite common for companies to outsource functions for which they lacked internal competency or resources. However with globalization, the scale of outsourcing grew far from outsourcing simply a few functions. In order to compete globally, companies needed to shed their bloated organization structures, and focus on what activities they really did well, and was the key reason for their existence; their core business. This gave rise to emergence of service companies that developed expertise and scale for delivering focused logistic services, financial accounting, human resource, product designing, data processing, plant security, maintenance and many other services.

Information Technology was the common thread that bound companies' internal as well as external global ecosystem together, providing the information visibility needed to make informed business decisions. More and more tools were created with the aim to enhance the integration of the new emerging complex supply chains. Collaborative Planning, Forecasting and Replenishment (CPFR) was one such concept that was initiated in 1995 by Walmart and the Cambridge, Massachusetts software and strategy firm, Benchmarking Partners.

CPFR aims at creating a shared inventory, and product replenishment information visibility among suppliers and retailers, throughout the various nodes of the supply chain. Planning and fulfilling customers demand through collaborative sharing of information between the suppliers and retailers is the epicenter of the framework. This allows flexibility in regards to the re-configurability of the supply chain, thus making the end-to-end supply chain process more efficient. Efficiency is created through the decrease in expenditures for merchandising, inventory, logistics, and transportation across all trading partners. So acting upon the extremely valuable insight gained by studying end to end supply chain information flow gave companies the competitive edge.

Information technology transformed the capabilities of Logistic function, enabled it to come out of silo and tightly linked with the rest of the organization. No one can argue the fundamental role of Logistics in global development, with the concept dating back to the very earliest civilizations. From constructing the pyramids in ancient Egypt, to the advent of postal services, to creating vital links in supplying military logistics during the world wars, to creating a competitive edge for companies competing in global markets today.

In the 70's and 80's, "Kanban" and "just in time (JIT)", the two manufacturing methodologies that migrated from Japan, had gained traction in the Western manufacturing world. The central theme of the two concepts was to eliminate waste associated with overproduction, waiting and excessive inventories, by producing to the customer's real time demand, and not in anticipation of demand. There was an emphasis on how the production of raw material needed to be procured, and it effectively brought in raw or semi-finished material suppliers within the framework of the model. This was the first time wherein a company's logistic function was effectively linked with the objective of the operations function. Logistic functions became the enabler to plan, implement, and control the flow and storage of goods, thus increasing the operational efficiency of the company.

In the 90's, globalization took off, barriers to trade were reduced, and thus the volume of goods flowing across international borders grew exponentially. The graph below shows the merchandize imports and exports as a percentage of goods produced in the United States.

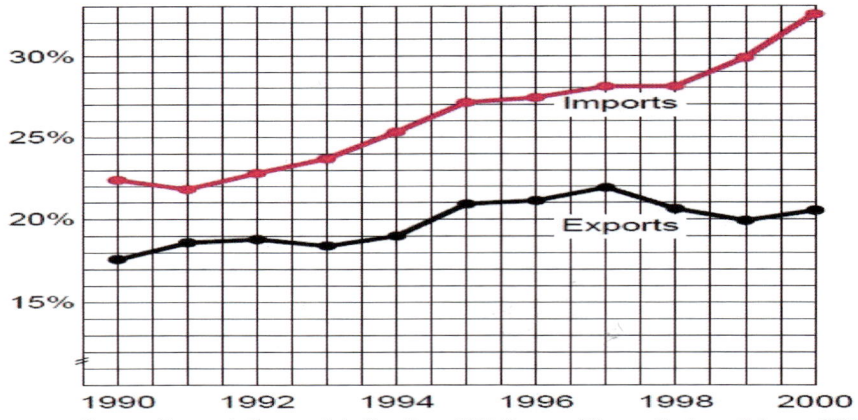

Sources: Economic Report of the President, 2001, Survey of Current Business, February 2001.

Outsourcing and offshoring, while on one hand allowed companies to procure products, and services at a much cheaper rate, also resulted in the lengthening of their supply chains, thereby added more variability and risks. And as supply chain length started to grow bigger and more complex, there was an increased demand for adding physical infrastructure and developing technologies for product transfer facilities.

Moreover, during this period, organized retail started to grow. Organized retailers started to expand to newer geographical areas, and carried an ever increasing number of products. Despite the challenges associated with short product life cycles, vast supplier sources, and limited physical space, these organized retailers kept surpassing and raising customer expectations by promising and delivering a wide range of fresh and cheap products.

Thus, warehousing started to emerge as a critical element of Supply Chain Management, as it helped to manage the product storage and control the product flow that was needed to support the globalization and growth in big box retailers. Quick response (QR) and efficient consumer response technologies (ECR) were developed during this time. These and other similar technologies allowed warehouses to move up from just being a storage place for goods, to being a center capable with being tasked with moving goods, planning and scheduling loading and offloading, and executing strategies that contributed towards building an efficient goods distribution network.

Moreover, a major breakthrough in technology that revolutionized the warehousing process and supply chain management, was the introduction of RFID (radio frequency identification; wireless use of electromagnetic field to transfer data). Though RFID was invented in 1940's, it only truly became visible in our daily lives in the late 1990's. As it allowed remote identification using a radio link, it enabled the tracking of movement of items throughout the supply chain, and thus enhanced supply chain visibility. This lead to procedural improvements now that companies could see the progress of their products.

Attempting to take advantage of this new technology, in 2003, Walmart convinced its top 100 suppliers to apply RFID tags to pallets and cases of goods that were sent to Walmart's distribution centers. Besides enabling tracking of movement of goods at various touch points, RFID enabled easy and frequent inventory counting, thereby improving the accuracy of inventory numbers.

Furthermore, this era also witnessed robust growth in the infrastructure to support the rising levels of freight movement through air, shipping lanes and rail-roads. Freight transportation by sea accounts for ninety percent of the world's freight movement today, and shipping companies own some of the biggest transportations vehicles on earth.

To put a perspective on the growth in shipping lane volume, compare the first container ship that carried 58 containers from Newark to Houston in 1956, to the data table below, that shows the annual data for the container port traffic (TEU) for just the top 10 nations from 2000 to 2010. This data is the measure of the flow of containers from land to sea transport modes and vice versa

Country	Year 2000	Year 2006	Year 2007	Year 2008	Year 2009	Year 2010
China	41,000,000	84,810,503	103,823,024	115,941,970	108,799,934	130,290,443
United States	28,300,000	40,896,742	44,839,390	42,411,770	37,353,575	42,337,513
Singapore	17,100,000	24,792,400	28,767,500	30,891,200	26,592,800	29,178,500
Hong Kong SAR, China	-	23,538,580	23,998,449	24,494,229	21,040,096	23,699,242
Korea, Rep.	9,030,174	15,513,935	17,086,133	17,417,723	15,699,663	18,542,804
Malaysia	4,642,428	13,419,053	14,828,836	16,093,953	15,922,800	18,267,475
Japan	13,100,000	18,469,710	19,164,522	18,943,606	16,285,918	18,098,346
United Arab Emirates	5,055,801	10,967,048	13,182,412	14,756,127	14,425,039	15,176,524
Germany	7,695,688	15,009,691	16,644,222	17,183,042	13,296,300	14,821,767
Spain	5,789,693	10,033,089	13,346,028	13,461,304	11,803,192	12,613,015

Data Source: data.worldbank.org

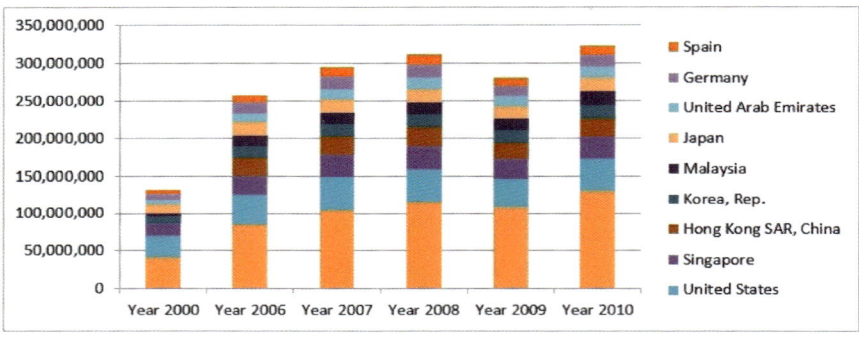

Thus logistic functions within organizations emerged as a new major source of competitive advantages and cost savings. Companies start to compete based on the effectiveness of their supply chains.

Moreover, the other significant contribution of Industries 3.0 was the emergence of "E-Commerce"; the merchandizing of products or services using computer networks such as the Internet. It took a while for governments to wrap their heads around the new online trading tool and to come up with regulations to deal with emerging online businesses. E-Commerce involved amalgamation of several enabler technologies such as electronic funds transfer (EFT; electronic transfer of money from one bank account to another), electronics data exchange (EDI; framework providing standards for exchanging data electronically), online transaction processing (OLTP; an IT system that facilitate and manage transaction oriented applications like bank ATM), inventory management systems (Software tracking products throughout the supply chain), M-Commerce(delivering E-Commerce capability in the hands of customer through a wireless device), and a supply chain management and critical data analytics frameworks that cut across all technologies areas.

Some of the early successes of this concept of E-commerce include Jeff Bezos, who launched Amazon.com in 1995, Larry Page & Sergey Brin who launched Google in 1998, and Jack Ma who founded Alibaba in 1999. These and other similar online based companies created massive disruptions for the traditional brick and mortar product and service delivery companies, and set the foundation for the emergence of the next digital revolution.

Industries 3.0 and Data Analytics
Industry 3.0 started with the ability to collect data, and then progressed to define meaningful structured data repositories called databases. Databases allowed users to define relationships between different sets of tables, and tools such as SQL query allowed users to interact with database and create custom reports. Soon, businesses started to rely more and more on data to view the performance of various key performance indicators, and plan necessary actions accordingly.

At the initial phase of data analytics, industries were trying to adopt strategies to deal with the new resource "data" that they had started storing on expansive pieces of hardware with low computation power. There wasn't a lot of data information that these systems could store due to technological limitations. The majority of industrial applications were aimed at enhancing processes for inventory planning and production scheduling.
Then, the birth of spreadsheets gave end users the ability to port data out to spreadsheets and perform data analysis operations for business needs. Spreadsheet programs saw tremendous evolution from VISICALC (1978), notably the first electronics spreadsheet program, to Lotus 1-2-3 (1983), that besides being a spreadsheet, offered graphical charting along with basic database options, to Microsoft Excel 1.0 (1985) that offered graphical user interface with pull down menus, and allowed for the use of a mouse device.

And then, in 1992, along with Excel 4.0, Microsoft launched "Microsoft Access", a DBMS (database management system) that provided users the ability to create relational databases using graphical interfaces. It also provided users the capability to import data stored in other applications and databases. Thus the end users' ability to do build simpler databases, perform data analysis, write simple queries in MS Access, and build simulations models using MS Excel spreadsheets, grew along with their appetite to do more with the data. Database structures thus started to become more complex, both as a result of the need to store more data points, as well as due to the higher computational power of the processors, combined with the emergence of newer database tuning and optimizing tools. This gave rise to complex multidimensional database structures.

Therefore, as databases grew multidimensional, newer tools like OLAP (Online Analytic Processing) were developed. These tools fell within the category of Business Intelligence Tools, and encompassed relational databases, reporting, and data mining tools within them. OLAP was an instant hit as it enabled users to analyze and interact with multidimensional data from multiple perspectives. As an example, different sales teams' data across multiple geographic regions could be aggregated under one sales division, and be used to anticipate the sales trend. Users could drill down and navigate through the details for a specific data point. Slice and dice feature would then allow users to slice (take out) specific data set, and view (dice) it from various viewpoint. Expanding on the sales example, this could mean that the user could view the sales performance by salesman, by time period, or by product performance in different regions.

Thus, the data analytics technologies made remarkable progress as personal computer technology enhanced computational power and larger memory at a cheaper price. This data analysis phase was more focused on executing strategies based on past historical data trends, and it saw a birth of a culture of data reporting, data mining, and dashboards of key performance indicators becoming the focus discussion points in board room meetings.

From the technological viewpoint, businesses had now established large enterprise "Data Warehouses" and "Data Marts" in their systems. Data Warehouses would integrate and receive data from all the data sources within the enterprise, and hence hold very detailed large information. Enterprise Resource Planning (ERP), Customer Relationship Management (CRM) and internal legacy applications are some examples of the data sources feeding information. On the other hand Data Marts allowed extracting limited amount of information from the data warehouse, and were meant to be accessed by the teams that requested that logical subset of the data. Data Marts set the foundation that enabled users to perform data mining, create reports and use tools like OLAP.

However, from the data analytics viewpoint, the analytic environment focused entirely on creating reporting using historic data, and the statistical analysis would take a painstakingly long time. Analysts would spend the bulk of their time prepping data so that a report could be generated. IT departments within the company were not tightly integrated with the other operational teams and any new requests for datasets or reports would have to wait for long amounts of time. As well, as companies worked with familiar customers and products, decision makers felt confident about their experience on customer and product related subject matters and would often supersede past data reports, choosing instead to rely on their intuition in such matters.

The next phase of Data Analytics, was tied with the emergence and tremendous growth of E-Commerce driven business economies. As the internet became incredibly successful in bringing consumers and businesses across the globe closer, more and more new products and services were developed based on the gathered customer data and analytics. There was a tremendous growth in internet based (Amazon, eBay, Google, Yahoo) as well as social network oriented companies (Facebook, LinkedIn). There was suddenly a flood of complex and large unstructured data information, flowing from numerous data sources, which were beyond the abilities of the traditional enterprise to handle. By 2010, the number of monthly unique visitors to Google stood close to one billion. We started to live in a truly connected dynamic world wherein information was flowing at light speed, and supply chains needed the abilities to re-configure themselves to meet customer expectations. Enterprises started to move away from reporting, and put their focus on predictive analytics, that allowed them to be prepared for changing environments and pro-actively gets closer to customer needs. New roles like Data Scientists start to emerge, and more and more companies started building products and services around data.

We ushered into a new connected world that day by day, becoming more tightly interlocked as a result of growing influence of internet and mobile devices. Technological innovation demands a new breed of knowledge resources for delivering a new generation of products and services.

Data Analytic Transformation Summary

HIGH	Reporting & Descriptive Analytics.	Utilizing & Acknowledging Data Analytics as source of competitive advantage. Reporting & Descriptive Analytics. Storage & Computational Technologies. Focus on wide variety of Internal & External Data source.	Cognitive, Predictive and Prescriptive Analytics. Seamless integration of Internal & External Data Analytics in decision making process. Turnaround time for Data Driven Insight. (sec)
LOW	Utilizing & Acknowledging Data Analytics as source of competitive advantage. Storage & Computational Technologies. Focus on External Data source. Predictive & Prescriptive Analytics Turnaround time for Data Driven Insight (months)	Cognitive, Predictive & Prescriptive Analytics. Seamless integration of Internal & External Data Analytics in decision making process. Turnaround time for Data Driven Insight (weeks)	
	Traditional Analytics 1970 – 2000	**Big Data Analytics** 2000 Till Today	**Future State of Data Analytics** Today and Beyond

CHAPTER TWO

PUSH FOR NEXT INDUSTRIAL REVOLUTION

"Technology is just a Tool; it's the People, who provide it a purpose"

From 1970 ~ 2009, Manufacturing Companies like General Motors, Ford Motors, General Electrical and Energy Companies like Exxon Mobil and Chevron, were the biggest wealth generating companies globally. Over the same course, Retailers like Walmart & Costco gained significant control over the fate of the manufacturers, and the world witnessed emergence of strong growth in the organized retail industry.

However, technological advancements, and their adoption allowed the IT industry to significantly contribute more to the world economy than traditional industries. The diagram below clearly depicts how technology companies consistently displaced and are continuing to displace traditional energy and manufacturing companies from their top spots.

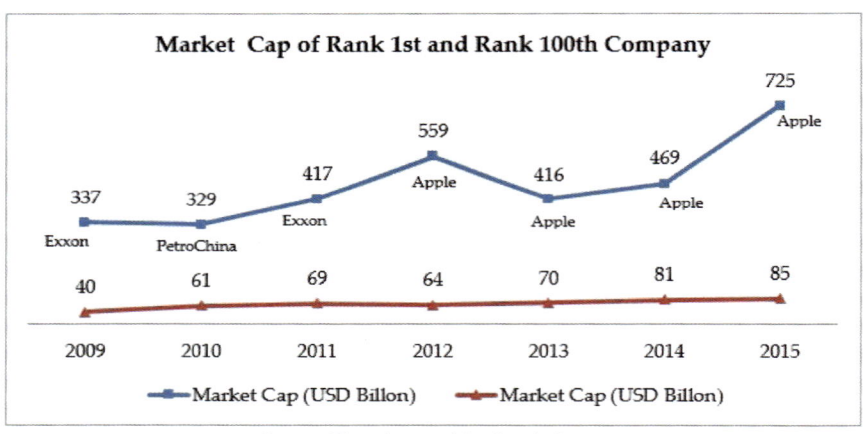

Source: Bloomberg and PwC analysis

Apple Inc, Google Inc and Microsoft Corp, hold the top 3 positions among the 5 top global companies in terms of market capitalization. Below is another interesting data set that shows the sector wise value distribution, for the top 100 global companies in the 2014 calendar year.

Industry	Number of companies	Market cap 31-03-2015 ($bn)	Dividends 2014 ($bn)[1]	Share buyback 2014 ($bn)[1]	Total value distribution 2014 ($bn)[1]	% of total distribution	Dividend as % of market cap [2]	Total value as % of market cap [2]
Technology	12	2,802	42	99	141	20%	1.5%	5.0%
Financials	19	3,236	92	21	114	16%	2.8%	3.5%
Oil & Gas	9	1,629	60	41	101	15%	3.7%	6.2%
Consumer Goods	18	2,529	73	26	99	14%	2.9%	3.9%
Health Care	18	2,632	60	34	94	14%	2.3%	3.6%
Consumer Services	10	1,516	20	34	53	8%	1.3%	3.5%
Industrials	7	844	23	17	39	6%	2.7%	4.6%
Telecommunications	4	722	34	3	37	5%	4.7%	5.1%
Basic Materials	3	337	12	-	12	2%	3.6%	3.6%
Total	100	16,245	415	274	689	100%	2.6%	4.2%

(1) Actual payment in calendar year 2014
(2) Market cap as at 31 March 2015

Source: Bloomberg and PwC analysis

The data above further substantiates on the changing industrial landscape led by the strong growth in technology companies. While Information technology was originally born to transform and enhance the productivity of traditional industries, it emerged instead as a powerful and competitive industry that has become the backbone of the world economy today.

Emergence of disrupting Technologies

Innovation in technology is facilitating changes in consumer behavior. In this section, we are going to examine the impact of consumers adoption of online technologies such as e-commerce, m-commerce and social media on businesses, and how businesses are adapting and re-strategizing with the changes and tapping new opportunities.

Traditional Industries witnessed enhanced capabilities within their ERP (enterprise resource planning) and CRM (customer relationship management) systems. ERP increased the efficiency of business processes by providing easy, standardized information access across all departments within an enterprise that helped in planning and scheduling activities. If one business area saw an issue then all the other impacted business areas would be notified, allowing them to take appropriate action and plan accordingly. It shifted the focus of organizations and led them to start managing data in order to track, analyze and plan their resources and activities. CRM on the other hand provided enterprises with standardized processes for collecting and sharing customer data and the categorization of outcomes from customer interactions.

In the B2C (business to consumer) sector, products such as consumer PC's and laptops, coupled with online connectivity made significant inroads for the e-commerce business. Consumers began using e-commerce to buy electronics, books, clothing, movie tickets and almost every other product and service available in the physical realm. Today, Google's search engine handles more than three billion searches on a daily basis, and helps online users to search for information from publically accessible documents offered by web servers. Search engines that started with simply providing information to consumers, transformed into critical data analytic sources for gathering and understanding consumer behaviors and needs.

In 2009, Google published a paper that described how a model it had created could detect an influenza epidemic by utilizing the search engine query data.

We are aware that seasonal influenza is a major public health concern. Every year it results in millions of people worldwide having to deal with respiratory illnesses and death. Some years we witness a new strain of influenza viruses emerging for which there is no vaccination available. The only effective way to deal with the issue is early detection that could help health authorities to take prompt response. Traditional surveillance systems rely on monitoring clinical data on regular intervals. Apart from gathering clinical data from physician visits, some countries collect data from the health triage phone lines available for the general public. As well, they monitor the data from over the counter drug sales. Traditional systems suffer significant time lag, and hence create a constraint on the ability to have prompt health response in place. Furthermore, tracking seasonal influenza is made harder in developing countries due to the infrastructure and awareness disparity compared to developed nations. As well, we are living in a connected world where people and products are consistently crossing boundaries thus allowing health epidemics to spread across boundaries with ease.

Google played with the idea of building a model to estimate influenza outbreak leveraging humongous online search data. To build and test the model, Google used five years of historic search query data (2003 ~ 2005) as well as publically accessible data from the health authorities in US, and estimated the spread of influenza across the 9 public health regions. When the result of the model was compared against CDC (Center for Disease Control and Prevention) results, Google model was found to be highly reliable and 1 to 2 weeks ahead of CDC estimation on the spread of influenza. Thereafter, Google has been consistently posting the epidemic spread by countries on their web site https://www.google.org/flutrends/about/.

Consequently, with the rise in internet connectivity and e-commerce, global trade barriers started to shrink. In effect, businesses started to focus on providing newer products and services to the mass global consumers as they realized the massive scale and economic benefits that they could reap in return.

On the other hand, consumers began to virtually connect with other consumers, and businesses around the world. They started to greatly influence the direction of companies' strategies around products and customer services.

Although it's hard to precisely quantify the business size of e-commerce today, a 2015 study estimate put it at around $1.6 Trillion US dollars. In fact, there are roughly 12 million online stores striving to divert customer traffic to their website. Online store number may seems staggering, in comparison to the worldwide retail market of approximate $ 24 Trillion US dollars; ecommerce is still considered in its early stages.

Ever since the introduction of smartphones, the world witnessed a surge in the adoption and growth of e-commerce. This extension was referred to as m-commerce or mobile commerce, a term that was first used in 1997 by Kevin Duffey at a launch of Global Mobile Commerce Forum. He described it as the delivery of electronic commerce capabilities directly into the consumer hands, anywhere, via a wireless technology". Mobile commerce services were first delivered in 1997, when two mobile phone enabled Coca Cola vending machines that accepted payment via a text message, were installed in Finland.

While PC's and tablets still remain the dominant devices people uses to buy and sell online products and service, the use of smartphones for carrying out online transactions are catching up quickly. Mobile accounts for 29% ecommerce transactions in US and 34% globally. However, in some countries like Japan and South Korea smartphones have generated more than 50% of the e-transactions.

Leveraging social media websites have become a critical component of companies' e-commerce strategy. Social media has witnessed such an unprecedented adoption that outpaced previous tools like radio, and TV. Worldwide, there are over 1.5 billion active Facebook users and over 316 million active Twitter users, who are sending over 500 million tweets per day. Apart from facilitating a sales transaction, Information Technology enabled social media platforms are defining a new unprecedented relationship between the consumers and the businesses. Today's tech savvy consumers through various social media platforms have created their e-visibility, and are able to influence Companies boardroom discussions with their opinions. However, besides simply using social media to increase brand awareness, find new customers, receive instant feedback and co-create new products and services, businesses are also heavily relying on using social media to improve their online communication strategy.

In the beginning, businesses simply moved the traditional "outbound marketing" concept of product and service surveys, and advertising on to the digital platform. It started to clutter consumers personal email boxes, there were banners, video ads, and display advertisements all over the web pages that most consumers did not find any interest or value, and rather perceived them as annoyance and interruptions. So despite companies spending a large amount of marketing budget on online product and service advertisement efforts, there wasn't much they were gaining in return, and rather had challenges in terms of measuring the effectiveness of their online effort.

Eventually, businesses started to re-evaluate their online communication strategies, and adopted tools to measure the performance of the effort. New "inbound marketing" strategies focus on engaging with customers, and moving away from pushing and merely displaying products and services. New digital marketing strategies evolve to address how to communicate effectively; how to get consumers consent before sharing finer products, and services details thereby earning consumers mind share, and have them be the trustworthy brand ambassador.

Social Media provided companies the much needed platform to connect, to participate, to analyze consumer discussions, feedbacks and act upon the insight gained in the process. Gaining insight and acting upon it on timely fashion is a critical success factor which cannot be accomplished otherwise without the help of the technology.

Plethora of social media data analytics tools have emerged for businesses to integrate within their business processes seamlessly, that provides holistic analyses of social impact on the business. I am going to mention few to give you understanding on how these tools provide value to the businesses.

Google provides a free web analytic tool that targets primarily to the needs of SMB (small medium business) online retailers having google account. The tool provides businesses critical insight into the behavior of visitors of the website. The tool also provides social media analytics capability that gives businesses insight into things like, how many people are discussing about the company on the social media, how they are perceiving them through "Like" and "Share" button, and what specific pages and content have been shared. The module once embedded within the company website, allows site visitors to share website content directly on their social network websites. As referral visitors starts to come to the website, the tool provides insight on how people from various social sites are engaging with your website. It provides statistical and analytical information helping businesses to focus their online strategies at right places. It results in providing better online experience and building relationship with the visitors.

Facebook provides similar analytical tool too. Unarguable Facebook is the most visited social media website, and thus making it an important platform for businesses online marketing campaign. Businesses can create their Facebook page and use it to interact with over a billion social media user community, and communicate information pertaining to their products, services, promotions, events and other related information. To help businesses understand how effective their online content strategy is, Facebook has provided a free "Facebook Page Insights" tool. The tool provides businesses tons of data points that help them to understand critical

INDUSTRY 4.0 DATA ANALYTICS

insight like; what posts people are engaging or not engaging with, number of people liking or unlinking the content, number of people commenting or shared post further, what time most people visit and read post, demographic statistic on the visitors and much more. Tool provides businesses ability to create ads, define specific audience they wish to reach, along with the reporting tool to help them manage and tweak the ad campaign.

Image Source: facebook.com/Microsoft/

A majority of companies have adopted multiple social media platforms for delivering unique purposes. A company might use Facebook to launch new product campaign, and may use blogs to encourage people to communicate back to them as part of the trust building process and, finally uses Twitter to communicate news to the external world.

Let's look at few real case studies to appreciate the new changing environment.

Case Study: Minecraft (Power of Co-Creation)

Utilizing social media to bring in, and involve customers over the various phases of product lifecycle has benefited businesses a great deal. Information Technology is evolving, shifting away from the traditional paradigm, where end users were mere users, and were denied to contribute their ideas for products and services development and delivery. In the new paradigm, products and services are enhanced by integrating end customers created context over the product life cycle. The beauty of the new approach is that it lets the end user community decides what new context or innovation idea would be adopted into the design, and thus making co-creation process an integral part of the design process.

Online video gaming is one such industry wherein this co-creation process is quite evident. Minecraft which is now part of Microsoft is one of the most popular video game that across various platforms has sold more than 70 million copies.

It's a voxel-based (voxel defines a point in a 3 dimensional space) sandbox game (sandbox is a computing environment to test new code without affecting the application in which it runs) that uses its user community to co-create various aspects of the game.

There are two categories of users; players, and another that are called Modder's. Modder's creates modifications or "mods" to the video game, and may upload the mods on to the community forums, generating discussions. There are several such online forums that exist, and Minecraft publishes a few of them on its website. A community game forum is one of the examples of co-creation which allows both players and Modder's to lean on advice from the vast community resource for in-game issues, game tips, game tutorials, developing and using myriad of free game mods that ultimately leads to generation of a better content.

Gaming video sharing is another co-creation process example. Each day the content sharing is growing by leaps and bounds. Both consumers and game developers are using the platform to upload recorded games as well to watch other players playing. In fact, YouTube gaming channels brings in around 4 billion view each month. On one hand it tremendously helps marketing of the gaming companies, on other hand it enables players earn money through advertisements.

Another area where co-creation is evident is in the concept of the beta testing stage during the game development process, wherein the company involves tester communities. Beta version of the software is released to a limited numbers of users that runs the application in real environment, and provide valuable feedback on product quality and reliability. There are several Minecraft Beta testing group on google+.

Today Minecraft is used beyond mere playing, and is finding applications in the field of computer aided design, and education. Combining the endless virtual 3D design abilities, and realizing it with 3D printers has the power to create unimaginable realities.

Case Study: Dairy Queen Enterprise 2.0 (Partner/ Supplier Collaboration)

Companies have started to emulate the success of capturing, and utilizing people contribution of collaborating and content sharing over the social media, within their own internal environment.

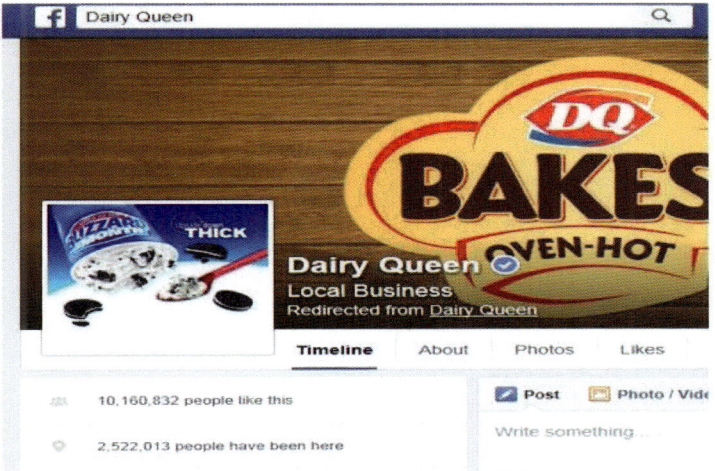

Image Source: facebook.com/dairyqueen

Dairy Queen (DQ) is an iconic chain of soft ice cream, and fast food restaurants owned by International Dairy Queen, Inc, a subsidiary of Berkshire Hathaway. As of end of 2014, DQ has over 6,400 stores worldwide, including 1,400 locations outsides United States and Canada. The product comes from the dairy farmers into the production facilities such as Dairy Cooperatives, where it's prepared and shipped directly in liquid form to various franchise locations. DQ manages demand and supply real time, and all aspect of supplier relationship on the behalf of franchises. One of their systems aims at establishing the promotional supply chain communication with suppliers. The system notifies suppliers about the upcoming promotion, and asks them to be prepared for increased demand for certain products. The other intelligent system iTrade tracks and manages the real time movement of inventory, by connecting and establishing communication among suppliers, franchisees, and the DQ corporate office. iTrade is largest network of food and beverage companies in the world, that provides technology platform for partners supply chains to collaborate on orders, logistics, and distribution.

GS1 is a neutral, not for profit international organization that develops and maintains standards for supply and demand chains across multiple sectors. DQ uses GS1 internet based Global Data Synchronization Network (GDSN) data standards, and uses iTradeNetwork's Certified GDSN Data Pool to share accurate, and timely product information across their supply chain. GDSN ensures that the data exchanges between partners are accurate, and compliant with universally supported standards.

Franchisees store sales information is loaded every 15 minutes intervals, and the system tracks the inventory usage tying it with sales, and orders with supplier. Franchisees simply uses smartphones or pcs, and connect securely using role based access to a cloud based application, and track the status of their orders, and delivery; interject and make changes to the order, or escalate if needed on the fly. The system collects data across various points of the supply chain, and using advanced data analytics tools turns it into valuable insights, enabling franchisees to improve their customer service, and drive revenue growth.

Case Study: TELUS: Harnessing Power of Internal Crowd Sourcing

TELUS is a 12 billion dollar Canadian national telecommunication company that provides a wide range of telecommunications products, and services such as internet access, voice, entertainment, healthcare, video, satellite and IPTV. Putting customer first, and enhancing operational reliability tops the corporate priorities of the company that employees around 44,000 employees.

TELUS always strives to find better ways to improve the wireless network experience of their customers by continuing to invest in the next generation network monitoring tools. The company when launched Automated Issue Reporting (AIR) network monitoring app, it requested for 25,000 employees to volunteer, and install the app on to their smartphones. The app designed to have zero impact on device performance, runs on the background of the device. It only gathers network quality data whenever it sees issues such as call drop, and service outage in real time. The app would then send the network quality data over the cloud securely on to the TELUS servers, and the data analytics engine would then summarize, and identify network hotspots for further investigation by the operational teams. These 25,000 employees scattered across the Canada becomes source for network monitoring data, and helps company vastly improve its capabilities to proactively manage its network, and fix the issues before their customer gets a chance to report into their call centers.

I mentioned the term "Cloud" in the TELUS, and DQ case study example above. It's a perfect segue to dwell into the Cloud technology, and help you to appreciate how it's seen as key technology enabler for digital supply chain transformation.

Cloud Technology

If you have an email account, you are already a user of Cloud technology. Cloud technology adoption is growing leaps and bound within both small, and large enterprise space. These days, it seems everything is happening in the cloud. But what is cloud? Withholding the technicalities for the moment, simply think of it as a place at the other end of your internet connection, where you can store your data, access and process apps, on demand.

The origin of the term cloud computing is indeterminate, but the term was referenced in its modern sense in late 1990's, and became popular after Amazon's introduction of Elastic Compute Cloud in 2006. As Internet connection speed got much faster - and more importantly, much more reliable - a new type of industry called Application Service Provider, or ASP emerged. ASP migrated companies' internal running applications out to their own or partner managed data centers. Amazon Elastic Compute Cloud (EC2) is a web services that allows business subscribers to cost effectively run application programs on Amazon's computing environment. Cloud providers buy computing and storage hardware and charge customers a subscription fee for keeping the application running. Cloud's central theme, is to maximize the effectiveness of shared resources and use the economies of scale to provide infrastructure capabilities to users and enterprises to store and process data in secured data centers.

One of the key advantages Cloud offers is the agility with which a business can automatically self-serve, and provision computing resources like server time, and network storage, without having to go through the human interaction. Consumers have the similar ability to rapidly scale requirements up or down, matching the demand and essentially pay only for the resources needed. Cloud service providers ensure that capabilities are available over the network, and can be accessed by heterogeneous thin and thick client platforms like mobile phones, tablets, laptops and workstations. Cloud service providers offer primarily three categories of service models; Software as a Service, Platform as a Service, and Infrastructure as a Service. These three different models offer different level of user flexibility and control.

Software as a Service (SaaS)

SaaS is sometimes referred as "on-demand software", wherein cloud providers manage the infrastructure, and the platform that runs the applications software and databases. The user of the service gain access by usually paying pay-per-use basis, or term based subscription fee. It offers the advantage to a business by eliminating the need for an upfront capital expenditure, and reducing operational cost of managing the IT infrastructure for running off-the-shelf application. Microsoft Office Web App, Google Docs, Salesforce CRM, Google App, Slide-Share App are some of the examples of SaaS.

Platform as a Service (PaaS)

PaaS providers provides development environment, and tools that users use to develop and run their own cloud applications, without going through the trouble of buying and managing underlying hardware, and software layer. Google App Engine, Microsoft Azure and Salesforce Force.com are some of the examples of PaaS.

Infrastructure as a Service (IaaS)

IaaS providers lets user run any application on the cloud hardware of their choice. So in order to deploy applications, cloud users install operating system images, and application on to the cloud infrastructure. IaaS comes in few flavors which is not in the scope of the book, however if you are keen you can read more on Private Cloud, Dedicated Hosting, Hybrid Hosting, and Cloud Hosting. Amazon EC2 WBS, GoGrid, and Rackspace are examples of IaaS provider.

Cloud Computing Influence on Data Analytics

Ubiquitous internet is the core foundation for delivering computational requirements for cloud computing. Thanks to the global enhanced network infrastructure, cloud adoption is on the rise. Global Industry Analyst Inc. has reported that the global Cloud computing services market is expected to reach US$ 127 Billion by 2017. United States remains the largest regional market worldwide. However, Asia-Pacific has the fastest growing markets for cloud computing services with growth in China, and India enterprise sector leading the pack.

As a result of growth in Cloud computing, Data analytics is also undergoing transformation to adopt itself to the new growing cloud data delivery, storage and compute medium. Cloud is always on, and the economies of scale are reducing the cost to load, and store the data. Thus, Cloud is providing businesses virtually endless storage and compute resources. Traditionally, companies were just sufficient to handle the structured data, however, Cloud provides opportunities to utilize previously untapped huge unstructured data that opens up access to hidden insights. Hence, companies started to evaluate their technology architecture to gauge if it could handle and store the volume, and variety of large unstructured data.

Let's spend some time to understand, what data is classified as unstructured data, and what some of the sources of unstructured data are. Unstructured data is a data that does not follow a specific format, and the traditional data handling technology didn't do much with it, except storing and letting it analyzed manually if needed. Like structured data, unstructured data is generated by both human and machines. Some of the examples of human generated data are:

Social media data

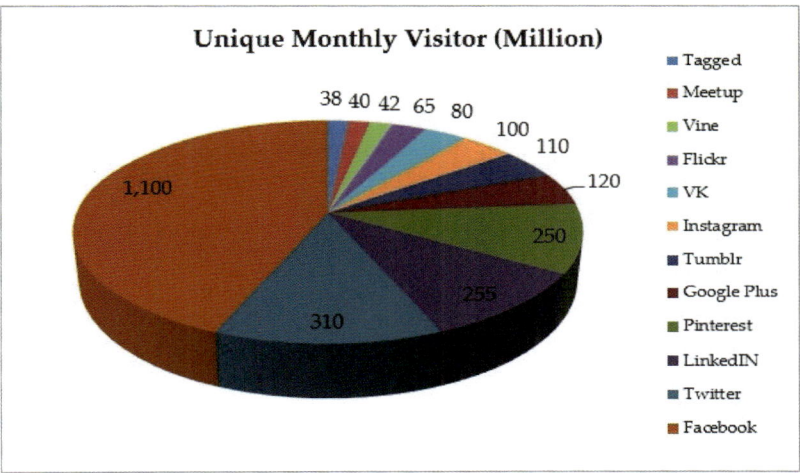

The above picture gives you an idea on the scale at which data is getting generated by the various Social media platforms. Over time, the data volume is going to get bigger and bigger. We should therefore thank Cloud technology that is letting us store this data on millions of different servers across the world, which otherwise was not possible. Businesses are using Cloud data analytics to interpret this massive BIG social-media intelligence data, and merging it with the business intelligence.

Emails
Emails and file services are one of the biggest contributors for the growth in unstructured data within Enterprise. According to the research done by Radacati Group, 205 BILLION EMAILS are sent each day in 2015, and by 2019 that number will increase by 20% to 246 Billion emails each day. You will be amazed by the amount of useful insight an enterprise can get from the

email data analytics. There are plenty of email analytic tools available that help organizations to improve the performance of email campaigns, by providing insight into how the emails been treated by the recipients. A piece of HTML code, called the tracking code, gets embedded within the body of the email or the template. Once it reaches the recipient, it starts to provide data back to the email analytic tool to analyze the aggregate data from multiple sources, and report enterprise with various metrics. Furthermore, data can be mapped to an individual email recipient, and hence could provide a much deeper analysis result.

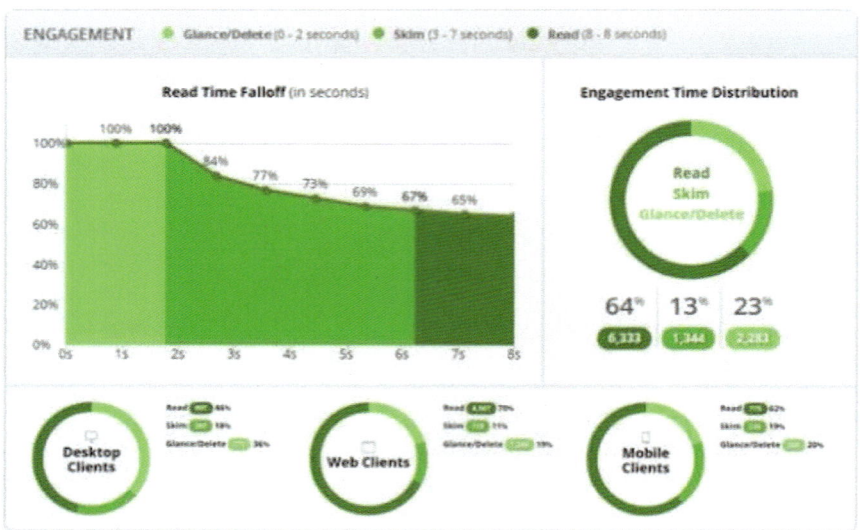

Image Source: emailonacid.com

Email analytics would provide companies with information, such as, how many people actually read their emails, versus how many deleted it. Companies are using this information to plan alternative strategies to enhance their email campaign. Once they know all the email subscribers who did not open the emails, they could re-send the email with perhaps some creative subject line changes, as there could be some distractions that prevented subscribers from reading the email in first place. For those who are merely skimming through the emails before deleting them, perhaps there is an issue with content or the offer that is send to them. In this case, company may want to reach out to the subscribers, requesting them to update their preferences, so that they could receive offers accordingly.

Data Source: emailclientmarketshare.com

Email analytics also provides extremely useful information on what devices email recipients are using to read the content of the email. Rather than advertise companies mobile app for iOS and Android to everyone, companies could use the insight provided by the email analytics to push banner, based on the device email subscriber is using.

Another important piece of insight the email analytics provides is the geographical region, where the email subscriber opened the email. In today's context, people are always on the move, and frequently switch places due to numerous reasons. Let's say the global retailer knows where the email subscribers are currently residing, they could trigger off an email to the subscriber, with offers for the stores closest to the subscriber location.

Mobile Data

Currently there are 2.6 billion smartphones in the world, and this number is expected to reach over 6 billion by 2020. Smartphones have already become the primary computing device for a large percentage of users. Besides making old fashioned voice call, users are using smartphone for SMS texting, instant messaging, browsing internet, social media apps, checking emails, streaming music, playing video games, watching movies or TV shows, using navigation services, mobile banking, and for many other activities. Video data consumption is the biggest driver for data usage. YouTube, and OTT (over the top) providers like Netflix are key providers for the video streaming data.

Let look at the case study of mobile data analytics, and appreciate how it's helping both the smartphone users as well as businesses.

Case Study: MOBIDIA Mobile Analytics

Mobidia, part of App Annie Company is an early pioneer in mobile measurement and analytics. It provides businesses useful data insight in areas like, App usage, Device usage, Network usage, and Plan usage.

Moreover, Mobidia being among the earliest app usage data provider worldwide, has accumulated enormously large datasets. Besides tracking hundred and thousands of other apps and mobile network worldwide, the company also have their own consumer facing app called "My Data Manager". The app, tracks and informs mobile user on their mobile data consumption, and helps them to manage data plan effectively, avoiding being charged overage. The app has several million customers worldwide. It gives company access to the huge dataset, providing useful insight into the mobile usage trend. The data is used in a manner to ensure end user information privacy.

Its App usage analytics, provides businesses with intelligence on app penetration, engagement and retention that are used to benchmark against competitor's apps. Furthermore, businesses use the result of the data analytics into making investment decisions process, as well forecasting potential advertising revenue.

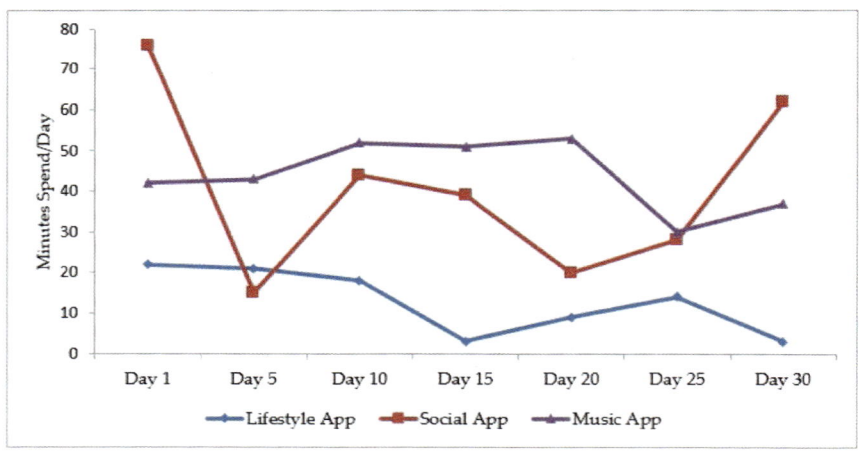

Its Device usage app analytics provides businesses with useful insight on customer app download, and usage behavior based on the device types (like iPhone, Android) and the screen size. The data is further easily pivot by countries and region.

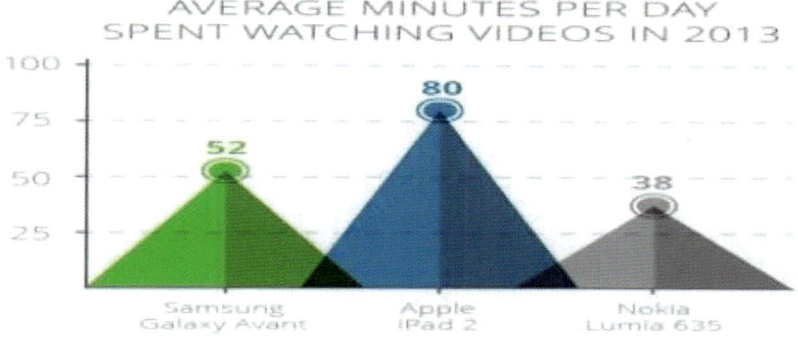

Image Source: appannie.com

Network analytics provides businesses insight into how smartphone and mobile users are using the network. This insight helps companies identify global trends relating to 4G and LTE roll outs, and plan their Wi-Fi strategies and public Wi-Fi roll outs.

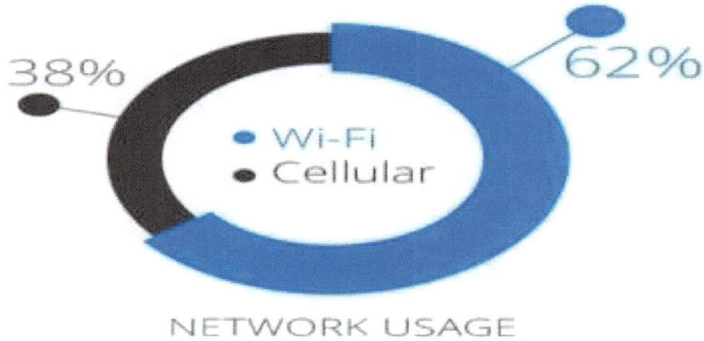

Image Source: appannie.com

Today, Mobidia services is used by over 100 top publishers, and over 400 thousand professional app developers working with 100 thousand companies.

Having seen some examples of unstructured human generated data, it's time to look at the unstructured data generated by machines. These days, we have more devices than human beings, which are consistently generating data. Let's look at some of the examples:

Security, Surveillance and Traffic Video Data
There are close to 250 million professionally installed, operationally active surveillance cameras in the world. Citing security reasons, several

governments around the world have carried out mass surveillance programs.

Image Source: i-hls.com

In 2012, Mexico City launched "Safe-City", an urban security system project, and installed two mobile command centers with over 8000 active surveillance cameras. The project was such a success that in 2014 Mexican authorities announced a new project to install 7000 more cameras, and panic buttons or 4300 points for emergency calls. As a result of implementation, there has been substantial reduction in number of offences, and large numbers incidents have been dealt in a timely manner. However, it's beyond human abilities to process the tsunami of video information feed coming from these cameras, and take timely action. Thanks to the cloud ability to store the massive data, and the advanced video data analytics, that is able to process both live and recorded data, provide real time critical insights, and raises alerts to the security teams. Video image gets converted into data, and based on sets of security conditions the system generates alerts, and make recommendations to users to monitor certain camera feeds. It provides users ability to perform searches for matching faces, or compare the images with government data to establish identities.

Industrial Internet of connected devices
Drawing a parallel between the online social media platform, Industrial Internet encompasses smart industrial machines connecting online, sharing enormous data. It is estimated that by 2020 there would be more than 50 billion connected machines.

As per Forbes 2015 ranking, General Electric (GE) is the ninth largest public company in the world. The company manufactures heavy industrial equipment's like jet engines, wind turbine, and locomotive. GE supplies technology that generates over 30 percent of world's power, and its engines runs from cars to airplane. The company is proactively monitoring these assets remotely to understand their behavior, performance, and timely interject to take actions when a red flag is sensed.

To stay ahead of the technology curve and customer experience, GE has heavily invested in Internet of Things, and data analytic technology. Few years ago the company took a stake in "Pivotal Software", a data analytics company that spun out from EMC. GE's Software Platform for industrial Internet, Predix Cloud which is built upon Pivotal Cloud platform, is the enabler for bringing asset operational efficiencies, by running big data analytics on distributed platform on the gathered data from the connected web of smart machines. There are millions of sensors, and millions of variables that GE Predix platform captures, and uses within the predictive modeling.

Also, GE is the world's second largest aircraft engine manufacturer, and these engines are loaded with various sensors that generates enormous amount of continuous information. Just to provide you a prospective on sheer volume of data that GE is tapping, one jet aircraft engines roughly produces over one terabyte of data per flight. Year 2014 witnessed over 100,000 flights a day worldwide; combining both passenger airline and cargo transport. Undoubtedly the scale of the generated engine data is enormous. By gathering and running the analytics on the data, GE is able to manage and repair jet engines proactively, curtailing minor faults from growing into a major repair issue. Furthermore, historical data provides them with insight into failure trends, and fault detection predictive models help to identify issues prior to them happening, thus driving huge cost and operation productivity improvements. By using Predix, Several of GE aviation customers stand to save millions of dollars in fuel cost. Airlines are rerouting flight paths, and optimized air traffic flow by extending the use of engine data from safety application to flight planning.

GE has taken a next big step in cloud computing space, and is expanding its Predix Internet of Things platform to provide Infrastructure as a Service (IaaS). GE is hoping to establish itself as leading IaaS provider, specifically catering to the needs of industrial customers.

Satellite data, RFID, MRI scanners are some other examples of unstructured data sources from machines.

One of the key transformations that we are witnessing in this new industrial digital era is adoption and usage of unstructured data, which previously was never captured or analyzed. Till now all insights driving enterprise were based on 20% of the structured data. Think on the possibilities once an enterprise starts to harness the power of 80% of untouched unstructured data.

Next, I would like to briefly touch on 3D printing which is one of the most promising disrupting technology that is pivotal to the Digital Industrial revolution. Later chapter will deal more on the topic.

3-D Printing

Amazon has filed a patent for providing services related to item delivery via 3D manufacturing on demand. The idea is to turn Amazon product fulfillment trucks into mini manufacturing units. A customer places an order at Amazon's website that immediately pushes the manufacturing instructions to the Amazon delivery truck, closest to the vicinity of the customer house. The truck completes the 3D printing and packaging of the product on the way to the customer's house. From simple toys to fully functioning cars, 3D printing allows for unlimited possibilities as to what one can print.

In fact, 3D printing has been around for so long that several key US patents have already run their term. Around 2009, printing patents that covered "fused deposition modeling" using plastics expired. Then in 2014, original patents on "selective laser sintering," which covered innovative printing using steel, aluminum, and copper, also ran out. Consequently, with these technologies now freely available to exploit, there has been a tremendous momentum, and focus on the 3D printing technology and material development for various applications globally. As a result, products can now be 3D printed that were once difficult to imagine, let alone create. As per "Statista", one of the leading statistics companies on the internet, the projected size of the global market for 3D printing, materials, and associated services by 2018 is expected to amount to around 16.2 billion U.S. dollars. These markets can be broken broadly into three segments; material, 3D printer and 3D printer maintenance. Data further shows that China, Europe and the United States are the largest markets for 3D printing.

3D printing process is often called "additive manufacturing" due to the reason that unlike traditional manufacturing processes, here an object is constructed layer by layer, thereby almost eliminating material wastages, and need for the expansive tooling investments. Cost-effective 3D printing is accelerating the mass customization of products in many industries, and big data analytics is playing a critical role in this trend. Both technologies are tightly interlocked. 3D printing uses visualization software tools such as CAD/CAM for modeling, and designing processes. With the file volumes going significantly up, there is reliance on securely store, and manage the stream of big printing data files. Also, in order to use 3D printer for a true industrial application, it requires real time integration of data coming out of sensors, printers, and other connected devices within the complex fabrication process.

Today's supply chains are super complex, processes are disintegrated, and are scattered across various time zones. 3D Printing technology in future has the potential to disrupt, and redefine the globalization/ localization equation. Additive manufacturing allows companies to build products when needed, and is going to diminish the advantages of outsourcing. We will re-visit 3D printing in the latter chapter.

Technology Adaption within Industries

In this section, I will summarize the essence of the discussion so far by splitting my explanation into three main sections; changing vision of the global industries, changing levels, relationships, and medium of B2C interactions, and finally repercussion of technology advances on the speed, and scale of technology investments by the companies.

Changing Vision of Industry

Products are losing value, and becoming commoditized. For that reason, alone they are not a source of sufficient differentiator in the marketplace. Consequently, Suppliers are moving away from the traditional practice of pushing products and services to buyers, and then sit and wait for the next capital cycle. Buyers on other hand, are no longer interested in focusing merely in getting the lowest acquisition cost. There is now a strong sense and desire for a far greater collaboration between suppliers and buyers on a regular basis to proactively, and holistically review the broad business, and identify points of opportunities where value can be added.

As a result, one of the profound changes all global industries are witnessing, is the transition of traditional product companies in becoming the provider of end to end solution to solve business problems. Here, Technology is playing the role of an enabler, for providing opportunities to deliver solutions for customers unstructured information problems, which previously was not possible. Companies are embracing new technologies. Even the traditional companies are now developing software, and data analytics expertise using both internally focused organic approach as well as by acquisition strategy. GE Chairman and CEO, Jeff Immelt summed this pivotal shift plausibly by his comment when he kicked off GE's third annual Minds + Machines conference 2014; "If you went to bed last night as an industrial company, you're going to wake up this morning as a software and analytics company". GE, the traditional Industrial powerhouse is pursing the goal to be among the top 10 software companies.

Big data and analytics are changing the landscape of everything, be it Governments sector, Entertainment, Sports, Healthcare, Disaster recovery, Manufacturing, Education, Energy or non-profit organizations. Predictive modelers and data scientist are now in high demand, as companies needs those skill levels to be able to use big data and advance analytics tools for making critical business decisions. The amount of data that crosses internet every second is more than the amount of data stored in entire internet 2 decades ago. Thanks to cloud technology, companies are trying to create value out of this big data. Walmart, American retail giant collects 2.5 petabyte of unstructured data from 1 million customers every hour, which is equivalent to 20 million filing cabinets. Walmart's CEO of global e-commerce stated "We want to know what every product in the world is. We want to know who every person in the world is. And we want to have the ability to connect them together in a transaction".

Future is going to belong to those companies that are able to effectively execute big data strategies, and thus by gain a competitive advantage.

Changing B2C Interaction

The new technology driven era has truly brought customer at the center of business ecosystem. Today's customers have highly visible identity, and their voices and opinions reaches company boardroom real fast.

How today's companies and customers interact, has seen a big shift from old traditional methods. New communication channels have emerged such as social media, emails, call centers, and web sites. There are far more real time interactions now, and customer's appetite for delayed attention to their response can cost a business dearly. Companies are expected, and are pushing to resolve customer's issues, and escalations faster to protect brand perception, and customer retention.

There was an incident wherein a group of black school teenagers were barred from an Apple store in Melbourne, Australia, apparently because of fear of theft. Someone at store, recorded the incident video and uploaded on YouTube that became viral. Social media sites have this virality phenomenon where content posted by a user catches attention of a large number of people across globe. Similar to a viral infection the news then gets further and further re-shared with other users. Apple CEO Tim Cook had to personally intervene, terming the situation unacceptable. He ordered Apple employees to be restrained on inclusion, and customer engagement practices. As a result, same students were invited back in store, and apology was offered in person.

Social media is redefining Businesses/Consumers relationship equation. WalmartLabs, a privately held company owned by Walmart has a big data analytic solution called Social Genome. Social Genome, analyses millions of social media messages, tweets, videos, blog postings, and more. It is used as valuable input by Walmart in predicting demands, planning supplies, reaching customers, and informing them about the products and special discounts.

Big data analytics technology continues to evolve and provide useful insights in helping companies connecting customers effectively.

Impact of Technology

With enormous growth in Cloud, Big Data and Internet of Things (IoT) technologies, businesses across industries are progressively evolving as technology, and data companies in order to stay relevant in the changing world. However, the speed of innovation driven by technology is putting tremendous pressure on the very companies who are in the forefront of coming up with new technological products and solutions, as well as the companies who are embracing these technological changes. Let me give you an example to explain the point.

Generally, supplier providing a business solution, charges customer upfront high CAPEX (capital expenditure) charges. After initial implementation, supplier solution support model would kick in, that then would lock the customer in paying 15 ~ 25% of the CAPEX as annual OPEX (operational expenditure) charges. Customers now have tied themselves by investing heavily in building supplier technology based infrastructure internal to their operation. Furthermore, Customer do not have any influence on supplier technology roadmap for the acquired solution. Hence, if the customer made a mistake in choosing partner, they would be stuck with a supplier with a poor execution of product solution roadmap and after sale support. It's also a common scenario wherein customer choose to stay with the older solution, due to lack of funds and resources to execute an upgrade. This causal approach is a source of severe ramification in the longer run.

With Cloud technology, the above described paradigm has completely changed. Cloud offers Customers pay as use model, customers are no longer tied to any hardware or software infrastructure or have to worry about keeping up with revision changes. The pressure has shifted to the solution providers. Solution providers are competing to stay ahead of the technology curve, by accelerating the execution of technology roadmap through building speed, and agility in the process. Agile innovation and customer experience has become the key to differentiate and survive. In past, engineers were coming up with new product or service ideas, but now it's the technology that is causing a shift in product design, and brining in innovation.

International Data Corporation (IDC) studies have shown strong growth in big data-related infrastructure, software, and services. A new forecast from IDC sees the big data technology, and services market growing at a compound annual growth rate (CAGR) of 23.1% over the 2014-2019 forecast periods, with annual spending reaching $48.6 billion in 2019.

CHAPTER THREE

EMERGENCE OF DIGITAL SUPPLY CHAIN

"The technology is available, the possibilities are endless, but the adoption is just at the beginning."

By now it must be clear to you that we have ushered into a new digital business era of ubiquitous cloud connectivity, unlimited computation, and storage of information. Billions of devices are connected together generating enormous amounts of data that is captured, analyzed, and used to make decisions real time.

In this chapter we look deeper on how companies are transforming their supply chains; how does a digital or smart manufacturing and smart logistic organization looks like? Towards the end, we will review the critical ingredient of this transformation, which is about building and inspiring data analytic culture.

Smart Supply Chain

It's evident that the technology has changed consumer expectation and behavior. Consequently, companies are striving to transform their supply chains from end to end, from designing and manufacturing a product or service to delivering it to the end consumer; every touch point is the potential candidate for the change. However each business faces a unique opportunities and challenges, thus within every business, there is going to be a different focus transformation areas and related investment decisions.

On one end of the spectrum, we have companies like GE that have head started transforming their supply chain, and on other end of spectrum are companies that are still wondering what would their Supply Chain 2.0 vision is going to look like. In our view, research from IDC explained plausibly on what are some few attribute needed for the new generation of transformed supply chain. They recommended a 3D value chain: "Demand oriented", "Data driven", and "Digitally executed".

Demand oriented essentially means, being customer oriented, being closer to the customer, listening to the customer, learning from the customer, and accordingly calibrating your internal business model to stay relevant. Data driven is about having tools and agile processes in place, to capture and analyze data almost real time, without much lag, and importantly having data analytical mindset throughout the fabric of the business, reinforcing fact based management decisions. Digital execution is about having highly visible, well connected organization, wherein people and tools come together super effectively to serve the needs of the customer.

IDC research further suggest that the 3-D value chain is both cumulative, and interconnected. What that means is, the demand orientation is a precursor to being data-driven, and being data-driven is a precursor to the digital execution. Let's understand how companies are adopting the 3-D value chain.

Take the case of Apple smartwatches. The smartwatch lets you receive, and respond to notifications instantly, flash warning about the weather forecast, monitor your heart rate, let's you pay for grocery, order an Uber, control your music with your voice command, and more of these functions without using the iPhone. Wristly, a research company, tracks apple smartwatch usage, and publish research material that any company involved with smart wearable, and wrist computing devices can use it. Its recent research found that Apple watch owners check their wrist 60 to 80 times, and majority of watch interactions come from time checking (20%), followed by notification (17%), and workout timing (4%). The data shows that users seldom read emails on the device. Apple and other smart wearable companies get valuable insights from knowing how their devices are getting adopted by the customers, at what rate, and what new use cases are emerging. It gives them a sense of where the smartwatch ecosystem is heading in the future, and with that knowledge they can tweak the smartwatch product roadmap, and focus on building a compelling mobile experience with the watch.

Another industry wherein we see a visible digital transformation is the Software Industry. In past, Software companies sold boxed software at a relatively high gross margin, that allowed them to pay for a costly distribution channel, which usually encompassed company own direct sales people, distributors, and Value Added Resellers (VARs). VAR performs more than just the role of a software reseller. They have sales fleet that covers territories not addressed by Software companies direct sales team, facilitate the license fulfilment to the customer, and importantly provides technical consultancy, design and training services. Since the onset of cloud technology, this paradigm is changing radically.

More and more software companies are now generating their revenue from cloud-based software as a service model, and boxes have either disappeared or become quite expansive. Cloud based subscription model is helping software companies monitor how customers are using their products. Understanding customer behavior, helps them to plan the content and timing of their next release. Companies now have more frequent customer's interactions through several communication channels like social media, email, call center, and website. On the other hand, VAR's having realized the coming threat are dramatically transforming, and establishing themselves into an engineering consultancy powerhouse, helping end customer finding, implementing, and migrating to the best available solution.

It's important to identify the relevant areas that are candidates for digitalization.

Note that the extent of digitalization of SCM within an organization depend entirely upon digitalization of the company's business model. Let me go over the various areas of digitalization, key levers, and challenges within supply chain management leveraging findings from the study conducted by A.T.Kearney. Study identifies four key areas for digitalization of the business model; "connected products", "embedded services", "product as a service", and "omnichannel distribution".

When we look around the products in our environment, we find one common theme among them; they are all smart products. They are no longer electromechanical products. Rather, there is a strong presence of various elements of Information technology within them. Products have complex hardware design, embedded sensors, faster microprocessor, operating system, connectivity, and data storage memory. Value chain that is needed to design, build, deliver, and service these smart, connected products is fundamentally different from the traditional products. Moreover, within the value chain there is now addition of completely newer activities such as product data analytics, and security.

Broadly, Smart product can be broken into three core elements: physical components comprising of usual electromechanical parts, smart components such as sensors, microprocessor, software, storage, and connectivity components such as port, antennas, and protocol enabling wired or wireless connectivity.

In smart products, software functionality re-configures the same product hardware to perform wide variety functions, thereby eliminating the need for additional hardware components. Connectivity module allows information to be exchanged between the product, its user, its maker, and other products in the ecosystem. Advent of Cloud technology has made it possible to decouple some of the functions to exist outside the physical device. An example of that would be Google Chromecast application on smartphone that streams media on to TV through internet connectivity. Hence, building smart products entails a company to build an entirely new technology infrastructure that however requires substantial investment. Furthermore, it requires a new range of human resource skills, such as software development, system engineering, data scientist, and cyber security experts, which are not found commonly in manufacturing industries.

Indeed, smart products are a boon for product manufacturers, and are helping to forge the much needed bridge to bring them closer to customers. Smart products are helping its makers to understand a lot more about how the end consumers are using their products over the life cycle. The insight helps them in designing new products, and proactively reaching out to customers sensing any signs of trouble with their products. Most importantly, smart products help product manufacturers reduce their reliance on the channel partners as it enables them to connect and provide services directly to the customers.

Smart products have led to an emergence of "Product as a Service" business model. The model aims at optimizing the overall demand for a product, by allowing its users to have full access of product, but pay only for amount of time they use the product. Zipcar has a membership based car sharing business model. It uses innovative data driven technology, providing customers with real time access to vehicle when and where they need it. Zipcar uses the collected users data to identify new locations to place cars, and optimized its fleet. Zipcar model has forced traditional automakers like GM, BMW, and Toyota to enter into car-sharing market. This wouldn't have been possible without the smart connected capabilities.

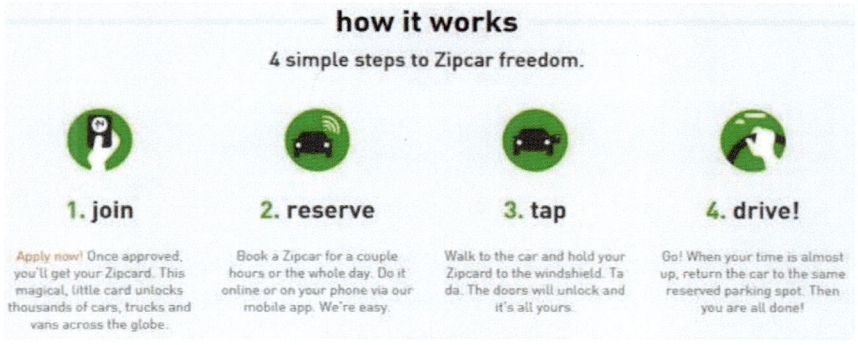

Image Source: Zipcar.com

Smart products are re-establishing new relationships with suppliers. Suppliers of traditional electromechanical parts are losing all leverage as parts are becoming commoditized, and more of hardware functionality is replaced by the software. On the other hand, there is emergence of new suppliers, providing smart components like sensors, connectivity, data storage, analytics, and other parts of the technology stack. These smart parts suppliers commands high bargain power, as they are the provider of a significant portion of the product value.

Smart digital technologies enabled omnichannel are driving the growth of anywhere, anytime shoppers. Along with newer opportunities comes newer challenges. Today's consumers expects information transparency, and trust when they interact with omnichannel. Businesses are striving hard to meet the consumer's expectations of this personal supply chain. Smart technology is helping them to provide consumers visibility on the stock levels, guaranteed service delivery levels, and a consistent hassle free return process, irrespective of the channel used. The same technology helping companies to create demand visibility, and build relationships with their suppliers, and logistic fulfillment partners.

Besides providing consistent demand visibility across omnichannel, companies are using digital technologies to involve consumers in co-creating value. Zazzle based out of Redwood City, California is an online retailer. Zazzle allows consumers to upload images, and create their own merchandise or buy merchandise created by other users.

Image Source: Zazzle.com

The company mission is: "To Enable Every Custom, On-Demand Product in the World on Our Platform", and are able to successfully utilized technology to encompass consumer in co-creating the value.

Some of the potential areas for digitalization within the supply chain to build and deliver the new breed of smart products, and services through omnichannels are supply chain integration, automation, reconfiguration, and analytics.

IT system integration remains the hottest topic among supply chain leaders. The area generally requires high capital and operational investment on continues basis, and is expected to create a source of competitive advantage for the company. Extent of IT System integration depends upon the extent of business needs to share data among the members of the supply chain, both internal and external to the organization. Integration challenges becomes complex, when supply chains are spanned globally. Classical candidate areas for IT systems integration within supply chain management are demand forecasting & planning, inventory management, capacity & production planning, warehouse management, network routing & transportation management, and interfaces with customers and suppliers.

Information produced by smart connected products and sensors embedded at various points, requires a new level of technical infrastructure that needs to integrate them into other business processes. Take an example of new generation of cars such as Tesla that come with innovative features. Tesla cars in need of repairs connects over the cloud, and downloads corrective software autonomously, or, if needed, send a notification to the customer with an invitation for a valet to pick up the car, and deliver it to a Tesla facility. Furthermore, implementing a robust security stack has become extremely important to protect the data, as most of these smart devices do not possess abilities to analyze security threats, and are prone to easy attacks.

Supply chain automation is another important candidate area for digitalization. Companies like Amazon spends a great deal automating their supply chain processes. Automation enables reliability, as the standardized process results are always repeatable and align with business goals. Speed, accuracy, and the ability to run industrial robots and autonomous vehicles 24/7, are phasing out humans from warehouses. More and more, robotic companies are getting acquired by large corporations, suggesting that the robot renaissance is on the rise. Attaching GSM or radio transmitters to products, packaging, or containers to improve tracking is another example of incorporating automation.

Air-France utilizing GSM, GPS, and Bluetooth technology is working to come up with the interactive luggage bag label, and a tracking device. The aim is to facilitate a faster and easier baggage check in, as well as to let passengers able to track their luggage over their mobile phone. Passenger needs to buy e-tag and e-label once, and register them online against their "Flying Blue" membership number. The idea is, prior to the flight when a passenger checks in online, automatically the boarding information would be sent to the e-Tag that is required to be attached outside of the suitcase. Since the luggage is now correctly labelled, passenger could now simply drop their luggage at the designated areas at the airport, skipping check in queues. E-track stays inside the passenger luggage, and provides luggage tracking information over the passenger mobile phone. Passengers also have an option to buy Samsonite luggage that comes with integrated e-tag and e-track. Qantas, the Australian carrier is already using similar concept QBag tags for the domestic flights.

Global supply chains are getting more and more complex driven by variety of reasons, such as changing customer expectations and changing operating environments. Designing appropriate supply chain structures and processes, to react to these changes are extremely critical to stay competitive and relevant in the market place. The dynamic re-configurability of supply chains is about having self-learning intelligent systems built into the processes. These systems are capable of assessing myriad of supply chain constraints and alternatives through sophisticated modeling and simulation capabilities. This allows decision makers to simulate various course of actions. The overarching goal for today's personal supply chain is to forge personal relationship with highly unpredictable tech savvy consumers. 3D printing is one such promising additive disruptive manufacturing technology that in near future is expected to help companies to forge that relationship through providing highly customized products nearer and faster to the customers. For now model of mass manufacturing in cheaper countries continues to be relevant. There is though emergence of micro-factories that are utilizing 3-D printers and other advance manufacturing technologies, to quickly build sample prototype products, sometimes co-creating together with customers. Once products gain traction in the market place, product production is pushed for mass manufacturing in places like China.

Big data analytics is a critical area that has the potential to bring the most SCM improvements, and has got most businesses attention. There is enormous growth in the volume, variety, and velocity of supply chain data. However, most of the growth in unstructured information is getting generated external to enterprise four walls, and is not supported by the traditional storage and computational technologies. Some of the examples of such unstructured, and semi-structured data sources are: consumers post on social media, blogs, videos, machine generated data, GPS based location data, weather data, traffic density, customer location, and emails records. Today's supply chains are complex and dynamic; however, technologies have enabled connectivity across the chain. The value is derived from holistically capturing and analyzing the exchange of information as a result of connectivity. Companies are investing in building big data and analytics technologies, driving intelligence and collaboration within SCM. Delotte study showed that prime areas that are seeing big data and analytics integration, are supply chain optimization tools, demand forecasting, integrated business planning, product tracking & traceability, and supplier collaboration and risk analytics.

Overall, extent of digitalization in businesses will continue to increase, impacting supply chain transformation. Though, the transformation will vary from industry to industry; however, new innovations will guide and create a much improved supply chain than before.

Digital Technology Enablers

A company's digital transformation at the heart is all about, tapping and utilizing hyperconnected world, leading to enhance customer experience. It's about capturing the pulse of new digital age consumers, who themselves are evolving amidst technology changes, and transforming steadily into a faster, agile, and better connected enterprise.

A study from World Economic Forum concluded that in G20 countries, GDP related to digital activity is worth approximate USD 4.2 trillion. It is about 3.5 times more than what the oil and gas industry generates, and is expected to reach USD 6 trillion by end of 2020. In order to match this growth rate, both governments and industries worldwide are focusing on planning activities around building infrastructure that supports the hyperconnectivity which is the fundamental to core of digital revolution. This would need innovation, and investment in mobile internet infrastructure, telecommunication equipment's, and cloud infrastructure.

Companies must review and address gaps in their current levels of hyperconnectivity, and this should be at the top of their digital strategy agenda. Hyperconnectivity is base to create the 3D value chain prescribed by IDC. There is no one common technology solution, however some areas or functions worth reviewing would be evaluating how your ERP systems is configured today, how well does it automate back-office functions; what opportunities and use cases exist for incorporating cloud computing and big data analytics solutions, how well you are exploiting digital tools such as social media, mobility to connect with your end customers and partners.

Cloud computing fuels the growth of the hyperconnectivity as it provides flexibility, scalability, ubiquitous connectivity that creates endless opportunities for companies to create newer platform for delivering business values. Every day new use cases are emerging across every industry, wherein businesses are creating new service solutions using cloud technology. Let's look at an actual example from the fishery industry, demonstrating how this industry is adopting cloud strategy to solve old age issue of dealing with reducing operational cost, balancing the demand and supply curve and thereby contributing to sustainable fishing.

Bari is a port city on the Adriatic Sea, and is the capital of southern Italy's

Puglia region. The sea provides local fishermen abundant supply for providing fresh seafood at markets, along the waterfront for homes, and restaurants, making Bari an important fishing area of Puglia, and therefore of Italy. On average, Bari fishermen handle 100 thousand tons of fish annually. It's a challenge for the local fishermen to anticipate how much of their catch is going to find a buyer, once the boat hits the dock. Bari being the tourist destination, makes the job of predicting market demand even harder for the fishermen. University of Bari created cloud based auction service application that connects fishermen on the boat with the buyer at the shore, and facilitate financial transaction. As fishermen retrieve their nets, via a touchscreen installed on their fishing boat, they enter relevant information pertaining to the catch. If they find the buyer over the auction, they start to prepare the fish for pick up while returning back to the dock, thus saving time. If the fishermen feel that they are not going to earn a fair price for the catch, they release the catch back to the ocean.

Similar to the cloud solution used by the Bari fishermen, the Pan-European network of Fish Auctions (PEFA) provides an online B2B marketplace in Europe that brings the sellers and buyers segregated by huge distance together. Northern Europe has vast quantities of fish which are caught by thousands of fishermen; however most of their buyers are located thousands of miles away in Southern Europe. PEFA has developed an iOS app that a buyer uses to select the fish auction of his choice, and is able to see information about the fish being traded (ship, species, time of catch, location, fishing method used etc.) on the screen of his phone or tablet, and indicates the required quantity. The auction clock app allows buyers to bid at thirteen different fish auctions in the Netherlands, Denmark, Sweden, and Italy from any given location.

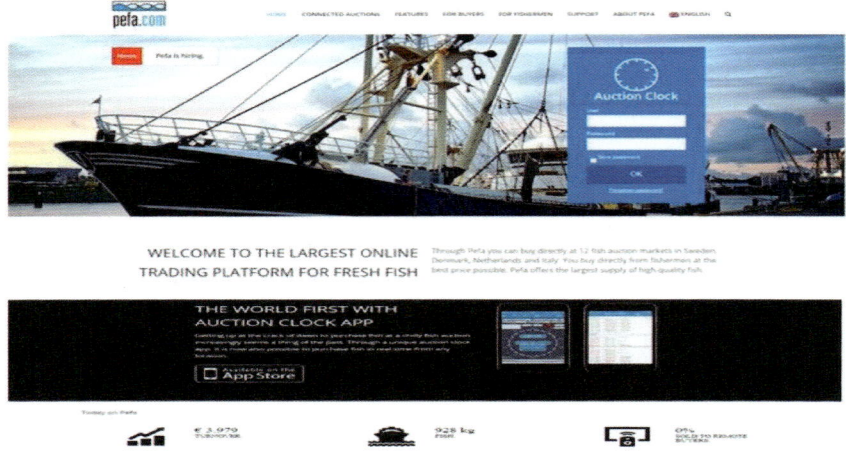

Image Source: Pefa.com

Now, I am going to briefly cover some of other exciting digital technological trends. More specific use cases will be reviewed in the latter sections dealing with smart manufacturing, and logistics.

IOT, Artificial Intelligence and Drones

IOT

Earlier, we touched the concept of IOT (Internet of things) briefly. All the three major technology trends namely CLOUD, BIG DATA, and IOT are tightly knitted. A key attribute of IOT is M2M (machine to machine) communication. M2M uses a range of technologies to create intelligent assets. Some of the key components within M2M ecosystem are the field deployed wireless devices that have embedded sensors, or RFID wireless communication network with complimentary wireline access. Depending upon the function of the machine, these devices capture relevant data, and have a potential to generate large volume of data (Big Data) that mostly gets stored on the Cloud.

IOT in Agriculture Industry

Advancement and hyper connectivity of smart sensors are impacting and enabling the transformation across industries. IOT is transforming the agriculture industry by helping it to deal with some of the unique challenges faced by the sector in the best possible way. The picture below provides the glimpse of challenges the industry is preparing to deal with.

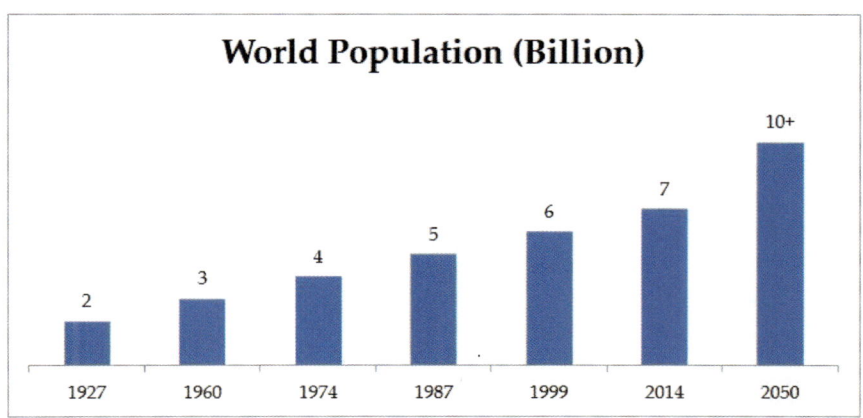

Amidst diminishing natural resources, changing climate, and compromised ecosystems, global agriculture industry is facing a major challenge of feeding an expanding world population. Food production needs to be increased by 60% from the current levels, in order to nourish the expected population of around 10 plus Billion people by 2050.

Interestingly, Agriculture industry is perhaps among the early industry embracer of the IOT technology. IOT applications are already helping farmers to improve the quality, and increasing the yield of the agriculture production at a reduced cost. Wireless, cloud connected network of smart sensors, and smart farm equipment's are automating everyday operations, providing real time monitoring, integrating data from external weather forecast, past historic weather logs, and providing holistic insights leading to smart decision. "Semios" is a rapidly growing company based out of Vancouver Canada, dedicated to developing safe and environmentally friendly orchard pest management solutions. The solution employs machine to machine communications together with a cloud database architecture. Semios goal is to eliminate the toxic chemical pesticides currently found in our food, and in our homes using precision pest management technologies. The pictures below explains Semios IOT technology capabilities that is available to improve the way crops are grown, and fields are maintained.

Image Source: Semios.com

Similarly, Google and FAO (Food and Agriculture Organization of the United Nation) are jointly working on a project to develop application that would help geospatial tracking, and mapping products more accessible. Using Google cutting edge big data, cloud computing, and mapping tools technology, the solution would assist nations to tackle climate change, and provide critical insight to experts developing forest and land-use policies.

In another use case, IOT applications are helping to continuously monitoring critical infrastructures of Oil and Gas Pipelines. Any loss or degradation of service may result in a significant financial or environmental loss. Embedded Smart Sensors in the pipelines are monitoring and providing data for maintenance, diagnostics, and repair.

Artificial Intelligence (AI)

Field of Artificial Intelligence (AI) is helping to accelerate current technology, and is behind the intelligence exhibited by machines, and software. Cognitive computing, a subset of AI, is behind creating self-learning systems that uses data mining, pattern recognition, and natural language process to mimic the way human brain works. Cognitive computing has already started to drive the evolution of global workforce. These smart machines, mimicking human brain are going to have disruptive impact on workplace. Though, on one hand it is increasing productivity and defining new levels of customer relationship, however, on another hand it is affecting the employment pattern. As a result, the future digital global workforce will witness a mix of human and virtual employees.

IPsoft, headquartered in New York City automates IT, and business processes for enterprises across a wide range of global industries. "Amelia", the name of their artificial intelligence platform, automates knowledge work across a broad range of business functions, and is already close to achieving near human cognitive capabilities.

Image Source: IPsoft.com

"Amelia", interacts like human, speaks over 20 languages, communicates with customers in their language, can reads and understands 300 pages in 30 seconds. In a help desk situation, "Amelia" can comprehend what a caller is looking for, ask questions to clarify issues, find and access information, and determine steps needed to resolve issue. If "Amelia" is unable to resolve a query, it instantly involves a human agent but remains in the conversation, and learns the solution through noticing how a human did. "Amelia" has already been used within many leading companies in areas like help desk, procurement processing, financial trading operations support, and providing expert advice for field engineers.

Drones

Drone is another exciting emerging technology. Latter in the chapter we will see how in near future they have enormous potential to play a critical role within logistic operations.

Drones or UAV (unmanned aerial vehicle) is an integral part of internet of things (IOT). Drones can be thought as unattended sensors that are connected to the internet. One among the numerous applications of Drones is the ability to use its integral Wi-Fi to provide broadband connectivity on demand to those places lacking necessary physical broadband infrastructure. Facebook has made a solar powered drone called "Aquilla" that has a wingspan of Boing 737, but weighs about one third of a Toyota Prius car. The goal is to use "Aquilla" to beam internet signals to the rural areas, lacking internet connectivity.

Some of other use cases of Drones that have become highly successful are:

- Drones use in environmental research: Eco-drones can access very hard-to-reach sites, are helping scientist to monitor polar ice melt, and relate it to the animal migration patterns. Drones are being used to study ice melt at a finer scale than satellites to study the impact of climate change.
- Drones use in wildlife preservation: In Mexico, authorities are using drones to protect against a reported surge in egg poaching of a threatened species of sea turtle that lays its eggs in the sand.
- Drones use in monitoring pollution: China is using drones to monitor air pollution, which is a major problem for the rapidly urbanizing country. The drones fly over power plants, refineries, and other emissions' sources to monitor potential pollution violations.
- Drones use in reforestation: Deforestation reduces 10 billion trees around the globe annually. Replanting trees by hand is slow,

expensive, and barely puts a dent in reversing the damage. A company called BioCarbon Engineering has developed a drone that can plant trees. Its drone uses tiny cannon to shoot seeds, nutrients, and fertilizer into the ground. The company wants to plant one billion trees a year using drones, and hope it will help regrow forests that have been destroyed by mining, agriculture, and lumber use.

Being a Digital Enterprise

As mentioned in the previous chapter, by 2020 we are expecting to witness 50 billon devices connected over internet. This interconnectivity of smart devices is going to transform the current state of Supply Chain. There will be a new ways in which the information is going to be tapped, and decisions are made. All these years ERP (enterprise resource planning) has helped transformation of SCM (supply chain management). Near future, IOT and AI are going to prominently become an integral part of the supply chain ecosystem. This will enhance ERP capabilities further by brining intelligence of smart devices and cognitive computing within it, leading to provide a new dimension to SCM.

Without a doubt, Technology is enabling organizations to transform from the incumbent hybrid supply chain structure into a more agile, and collaborative digital supply chain. An organization executing digitally will be fast, effective, closer to the customer, and in possession of highly accurate data. Silo disconnected operation initiatives have no place in the new digital economy. Though technology is key enabler, however, digital transformation is fundamentally more about an enterprise-wide transformation and less about implementing technology.

Smart Manufacturing

Though not every region of world is witnessing a growth in the population, however, overall world population is growing. It is expected that over next 15 years, markets would see an additional 1 billion new consumers. This translates to tremendous opportunities for businesses, if they are able to successfully attract these new customers. However, this also means that companies have to enhance existing capabilities, competencies, and achieve newer efficiency levels. Manufacturing industry is undergoing rapid evolution to address the gaps in manufacturing new generation of smart products and embracing new technologies. Besides, it is getting ready to address complexities with growing consumer's base, and other supply related challenges.

Smart manufacturing at the core is about applying information to increase the manufacturing intelligence, integrating customer voice throughout the manufacturing supply chain, and maximizing environmental sustainability. This entails a coordinated, and performance oriented manufacturing, that is able to reconfigure its supply chain in a heartbeat to respond to customer changing needs. Manufacturing traditionally been a data driven entity that depends heavily on capturing, and performing statistical analyze of data. However exponential growth in information technology is creating rich information driven environment that is spanning factories, distributing centers, and other areas of the chain. Consequently, the data requirements have changed, and so are the methods to capture and analyze data. Technological innovation in manufacturing is allowing diverse machines and equipment's to communicate seamlessly, generating richer context data that's opening newer opportunity to simulate, optimize, and control manufacturing processes. Data driven smart tools are being used to design and build products, operate, maintain, manage industrial facilities that significantly increases efficiency, and reduces waste. Conversely, protection of proprietary data, system interoperability, and cyber security are some of the new challenges that have emerged in digital manufacturing.

Besides Information Technology, Innovation in material sciences especially in the field of nanomaterials, biotechnology, and lightweight materials are resulting in development of promising newer industrial and consumer applications, driving adoption for enhanced capabilities in manufacturing.

Let's dwell upon some areas, driving innovation in the manufacturing industry.

Innovation in product design
Changing customer expectations in the personalized world has impacted product design methodology.

As discussed before, new product designs now have added complexities, as designers have to combine the physical and the digital elements along with enabling product cloud connectivity. Some of the key product design goals are:

Design for continuous improvement: Unlike old sequential product design methodology, wherein products were designed in discreet generations, and flaws and improvements would then get incorporated in the next generation, Smart products are designed for continuous improvement. Smart product design incorporates additional hardware and software design capabilities to track product health, and performance data. Network connectivity element helps to remotely upgrade smart products features, and flaws on a continuous basis via software. Software design has replaced, decoupled, and owned lot of features and functionalities reliance from the physical hardware layer. From getting software update on our iPhone for iOS or the installed app, to remotely upgrading the firmware of the server running in a datacenter, we are clearly witnessing the element of design for continuous improvement. The goal is to make products perform better and better over its life cycle.

Design for system interoperability: As smart products becoming part of the larger systems, interoperability becomes supreme important. Interoperability in design is an approach on how your product would communicate and exchange data with other products, using heterogeneous software, networking technologies, and protocol. Companies have to incorporate decisions in design on if they would be building just a discrete standalone product, or create a product platform that cuts across all related products and brands. From consumers perspective they would value interoperability in order to preserve in time the value of their investment. There are several parallel initiative such as DG Connect (European Commission Directorate General) working on creating standards for smart products interoperability.

Design for security and privacy: Connectivity in the smart product is designed to allow sharing and storing of information. However we live in a world of constant security threats and cyber-attacks. FBI sometimes ago issued a public service announcement warning businesses and homeowners on the vulnerability for malicious cyber-attack on their web-based connected devices like smart HVAC systems, security cameras, alarms, smart medical devices such as heart beat monitor, Thermostat, wearable devices, smart appliances, and smart devices to control TV or fuel monitoring systems. Besides low consumer security awareness, the other big challenge with most smart devices and sensors is the missing security capabilities, and patching vulnerabilities. These pitfalls were largely responsible for the security breach at US retailer Target, wherein 40 million credit, and debit card data was stolen. Hackers gained access to Target network by using login credentials stolen from a company that provides HVAC (heating, ventilation and air conditioning) services to the retailer. Amidst growing security concerns, there is an unprecedented involvement of IT security in designing smart products. Smart products consumers are getting more and more concern, and sensitive about protection and privacy of their personal, and sensitive data on the device. Company's ability to build a secured product is going to be a key source of competitive differentiation.

Design for new business models: Smart connected products is providing options to businesses on how they want to deliver value to the end consumers; either through a product or through product as a service. Philips lighting has made its foray into offering "lighting as a service" model, an innovative ways allowing facilities to install relatively-expensive solid-state lighting (SSL) without incurring high upfront costs. In one such deal, Philips is going to supply new lighting for the terminals at the Netherlands Schiphol Airport. Philips will continue to own the light equipment's, and Schiphol Airport will pay for the light used. Philips will get paid from the savings the SSL are expected to provide each year. Intelligent connected lighting system provides remote monitoring for detection of faults and failures. Additionally, system will control the LED output through smart controls, taking into consideration the amount of natural light available, and passenger's traffic flow.

In essence, Product design now has become a system engineering problem. Design changes in one discipline have impacts on the designs in other disciplines. Hence, product design demands an increased collaboration and synchronization across disciplines, across businesses in design, test, and validation phases of the product. Recently Ericsson (communication and technology service provider), E.ON (energy company), and ABB (power and automation specialist) have come together, and signed a cooperation agreement to develop innovative products and services to deliver smart energy solutions for a number of industries, helping businesses reduce energy and operation costs, and improve consumers' comfort and productivity.

Thus, innovations in product design are driving manufacturing companies to build newer capabilities, and collaborate with new partners across industries.

Innovation in production processes
McKenzie study has shown four key trends that are affecting production processes and platform design in manufacturing industries:

1. Digital modeling, simulation and visualization
2. Robotics
3. Additive manufacturing
4. Green manufacturing

Digital modeling, simulation and visualization

Digital technology has made it possible to create the digital image of the product that simulate the design virtually, thereby replacing the need to build a physical prototype. Powerful 3D software further helps with visualization, and simulation of production lines. Visual Component, headquartered in Finland provides suit of software applications for manufacturers, machine builders, and system integrators. Its 3D software are used in multiple business areas such as simulation and visualization of factory, production lines, complex robotic, work cell, and more. Software allows users perform visualization in all stages of production line design, from the very initial design stage to rearranging, or adding additional machines to existing production line, or even when there is no data available to describe the concept. The 3D simulation tools help designers to virtually build, run, test performance of the production lines, thereby has a significant positive impact on the product and process development cost, and the time to market. Automobile companies are consistently saving millions of dollars, ever since they adopted digital mock-ups for designing cars. Before the vehicle production goes live, production engineer's conducts 3D assessments to test part assemblies and other aspects.

Robotics

Year 2014 witnessed 29% sales growth in worldwide industrial robots totaling 229,261 units. This is by far the largest year over year sales increase robotic industry has seen.

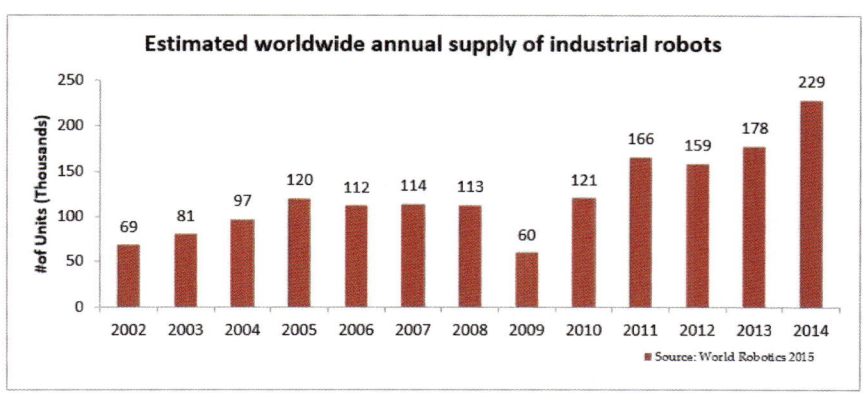

Future years, industrial robot sales trend is expected to continually grow upwards. The World Robotics 2015 Statistics issued by International Federation of Robotics (IFR) predicts from 2018 onwards, a year over year growth of 15% in the average robot sales. Report further showed that automotive part suppliers and electrical and electronics industry are the biggest adopter of the robotic technology.

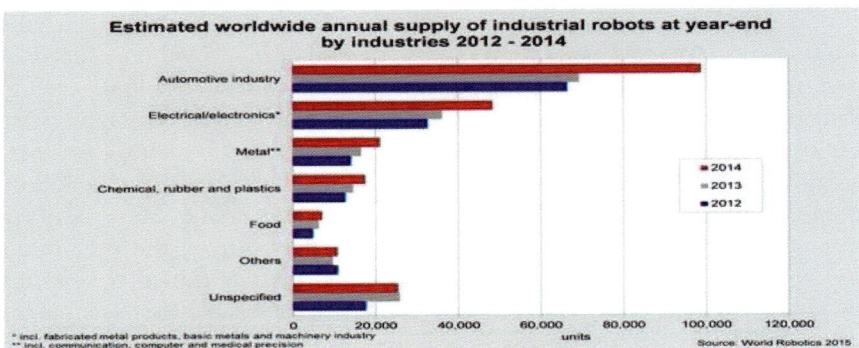

In terms of geography, reports shows Asia is the leading market for industrial robots, followed by Europe. Japan continue to lead in terms of robot density in the automotive industry with 1,414 industrial robots installed per 10,000 employees, followed by Germany with 1,149, and the United States with 1,141.

There are numerous reasons for using industrial robots, ranging from enhancing the velocity of repetitive process, reducing process variability, increasing quality for complex processes, and getting around ergonomic restrictions. Material handling, complex wielding operations, and machine assembly are the three top industrial areas where robots are contributing immensely.

Moreover, due to pricing affordability, simplification in use, and advances in artificial intelligence, robotic applications are finding adoption within SMB space too. "Rethink Robotics" is among the 2015 top 50 smartest company per the MIT technology review. The company has built a new generation of smart, high performance collaborative robot "Sawyer".

Image Source: RethinkRobotics.com

Sawyer is designed for machine tending, circuit board testing, and other precise industrial tasks that are not practical to automate with traditional industrial robots. These robots do not need safety cages, complex programming or costly integration, and are providing companies cost effective ways to meet dynamic customer requirements. Robotics will come to play a bigger role in providing flexible automation which is the key priority in manufacturing industries, including low cost regions.

Additive manufacturing

It is the process of making physical objects from 3D model data by joining materials layer by layer, as opposed to subtractive manufacturing methodologies, such as traditional machining. Additive manufacturing encompasses several technologies such as laser sintering, stereo lithography, FDM (fused deposition modelling), and many more. 3D printing is widely used by Industry to build product rapid prototype and functional models. As 3D printer technology getting advanced and is able to work with a wide range production-grade plastics and metals, the 3D industrial machines are increasingly being used to make final production products too.

The "Strati" from Local Motors is considered to be the first 3D printed car whose retail purchase will be available in tail end of 2016. As per company released information nearly all of the body panels and chassis are 3D printed. Overall, roughly 75% of the car bill of material is 3D printed. The company is using 80% of ABS plastic, and 20% of carbon fiber. Local Motors have partnered up with IBM to integrate IoT technology through IBM cognitive technology Watson into the 3D printed car, and SABIC to improve materials.

Additive manufacturing is helping to create new business models. "Spare parts on demand" is one such emerging business model that is seeing a tremendous traction from the market. Traditional spare part business model is highly complex and expensive. Original equipment makers (OEM) have high reliance on suppliers and wholesalers to build, stock, and deliver spare parts to end customers. There is a tremendous overhead associated with spare parts forecasting, warehousing, distribution planning, inventory management, reverse logistics, and packaging. Ultimately, Customers have to bear the brunt of high spare cost and long delivery lead times. Printing of spare parts on demand has a potential to transform manufacturing, as it reduces traditional business processes cost, leading to lowers spare part cost and quick product turnaround. Also, argument of traditional economies of scale is losing ground, as 3D printing allows for a great deal of design customization, and forging the gaps between the manufacturer and the end customer.

It's just the beginning, Additive manufacturing has a huge potential to revolutionaries manufacturing, and the technology advancement will further create new innovative applications and increased adoption.

Green manufacturing

Driven by the continuous business pressure on operations to eliminate inefficiencies and improve productivity, manufacturing techniques and frameworks are continuously evolving. It's always been about increasing processing time, removing wastages, and adding economic values. Manufacturing has evolved from mass production, flexible production to smaller batch production, and is now transitioning into what is called sustainable production.

As per the definition used by United Nation, "Sustainable development is the development that meets the needs of the present, without compromising the ability of future generations to meet their own needs". Hence, Green or sustainable manufacturing is about incorporating metrics, measures, and control on the impacts made by the actions of downstream and upstream activities on Environment, Society, and Economy.

The Ricoh Company, Ltd. is a Japanese multinational imaging and electronics company. The company strives to be a total sustainable corporation, and each of its product begins and ends in recycling and reuse of material.

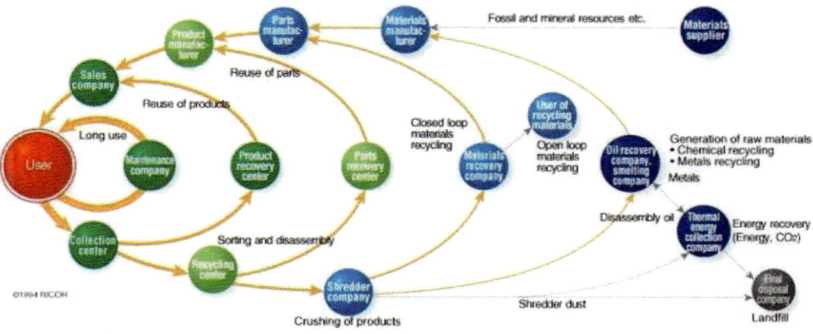

The above "Ricoh Comet Circle" diagram provides holistic view of all end to end activities, and resources needed to fulfill their sustainable strategy. Forward or Upstream supply chain activities depicts material supply chain; how materials gets converted into a useful parts that gets fitted into a product, which is then flown to the end user through the company's sales channel. Bottom portion depicts various activities coming out from the User. The idea is that more direct the resources are returned back to user, lesser energy is needed, and greener the process is. The success of reverse supply chain is dependent upon the design of the forward supply chain as that would dictate how tight the reverse supply chain loop is to the user. All of the Ricoh Electronics facilities are certified "Zero Waste to Landfill" that means a 100% resource recovery rate, and no waste makes it to the landfill.

Undoubtedly, addressing the needs for the Environmental and the Social issues are gaining momentum, as both customers and governments are demanding industries of the world to pay attention. Tougher regulations are pushing penalties, and tax implication for breaches are forcing companies to change the way business is done.

Dow Jones Sustainability Indices (DJSI) evaluates the sustainability performance of the largest 2,500 companies listed on the Dow Jones Global Total Stock Market Index based on an analysis of corporate economic, environmental, and social performance. It assess issues such as corporate governance, risk management, branding, climate change mitigation, supply chain standards, and labor practices. The goal is to encourage companies to improve execution of their sustainable strategies, and at the same time remove companies that do not operate in a sustainable and ethical manner. As on October 6, 2015, Volkswagen AG (VW) was removed from the Dow Jones Sustainability Indices (DJSI). A revelation of manipulated emissions test triggered investigation. DSJI upon reviewing the issue decided to remove the Company from the DJSI World, the DJSI Europe, and all other DJSI indices.

Innovation in the manufacturing information system

Within various aspects of manufacturing, applications based on technologies like Internet of Things (IoT), big data analytics and social media have started to appear.

Usually, there is no dearth of operational and shop floor data on the manufacturing floor. Applying big data analytics on the data, is helping to streamline manufacturing value chain by finding the vital elements of process performance, and then taking actions to persistently improve them.

In pharmaceutical industries, it is common to take anywhere from 10 to 15 years of painstaking work, before a vaccine hits the market. Besides the long research process, manufacturing a vaccine involves use of live genetically engineering molecules, which is a highly complex process that must satisfy the regulatory approved manufacturing process. Else, the medical and legal implications could have devastating impact on customers and the company. Research from IDC manufacturing insight estimates, on average, manufacturer sacrifice between 200 and 400 basis points in margin to poor quality. Pharmaceutical industry giant Merck was witnessing lower than usual yield rate on certain vaccines. Merck implemented big data analytics solution that ran 15 billion calculations, 5.5 million batch-to-batch comparisons, and resulted in pointing to certain characteristics in the fermentation phase of vaccine production responsible for the poor yield.

Big data and advanced analytics is already been used to optimize manufacturing production schedules, taking in insights from suppliers, customers, machine availability, equipment, and cost constraints thus acting as catalyst in bringing IT, manufacturing, and operational systems together.

Similarly, Social media is another great resource for manufacturing companies to share and promote their brand story. Manufacturers are posting on YouTube diverse videos ranging from story behind their brand history, advertising, and educational industry content videos.

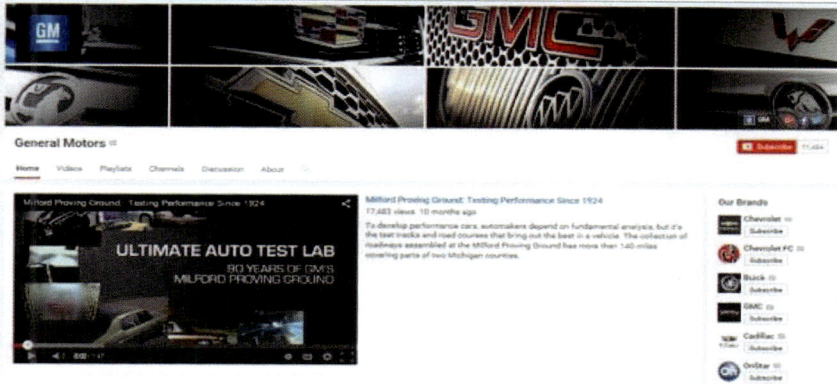

Image Source: Youtube.com/user/gmblogs

Companies such as Facebook, LinkedIn are allowing businesses to create a business profile, boost their social presence, and establish business connections through networking. Similarly, Twitter and Facebook are effective ways to connect with customers, and gather customer feedback on product quality and other related things.

Image Source: Youtube.com/user/TeslaMotors

Internet of Things (IoT) based web of sensor technologies are driving collaboration among the cyber physical systems, and creating new opportunities in manufacturing space. IoT allows to tap in, and share real time data from various sensors installed on the assembly lines back to the production team. The information helps to fills the huge gaps about the real-time conditions of the production lines, and hence makes it possible to further optimize production. Essentially, IoT in manufacturing is allowing factory workers to communicate with machines real time, thereby creating a visible connected enterprise.

We will witness more and more factories adopting information technologies that binds them enterprise wide to create efficient, productive, and smarter digital factories.

Dev-Ops

Smart products are becoming more and more software intensive. A new buzzword "DevOps" that originated from the software industry is slowly finding its way in the manufacturing world. It describes the approach based on the principles of lean and agile collaborative development, bringing cross-functional stakeholders, and customer's inputs together to deliver software.

DevOps framework holds paramount importance in the realm of evergreen product design, manufacturing, service support, and product upgrades. Usually, DevOps team consist of software engineering experts from the product development team ("Dev") and members from IT, manufacturing, and service who are responsible for the operation ("Ops") side of the product. In this approach, product capability is enhanced incrementally, and customer feedback is received quickly as possible. The DevOps principles are breaking the traditional barrier between product development, and operational team's, thereby fostering trust and communication.

Smart Manufacturing Challenges

A number of big companies are already beginning to tap into few of many faucets of smart manufacturing goals, however there are numerous challenges that first need to overcome before we could witness a mass scale industry wide adoption.

Below are some of the barriers that are preventing a lot of companies to embrace smart technologies in manufacturing:

1. High capital cost of acquiring software, and customizing tools for each plant.
2. Lack of industry specific standardized platforms/ software that can be easily ported.
3. High cost of sensors plus lack of ability to adapt many different environments.
4. Lack of standardized, efficient industrial data collection, and management methods for the comprehensive sensor networks.
5. Lack of standards, tools for integrating product and manufacturing process models by industry.
6. Concerns over protection of intellectual property as a result of

enterprise-wide integration
7. Lack of appropriate trained tech-savvy workforce to ensure successful implementation, and maintainability of new technologies.

To address these challenges, SMLC (smart manufacturing leadership coalition), a non-profit organization which is recognized for its leadership in Smart Manufacturing is building open smart manufacturing platform. The open platform would enable manufacturing companies in US to gain easy, affordable access to modelling, and analytical technologies that can be tailored to meet cross-industry business-case objectives, without having to retrofit existing systems. SMLC identified ten actions within four categories as priorities to move Smart Manufacturing into a broader spectrum of industrial sector.

1. Industrial community modeling and simulation platforms for smart manufacturing
   a. Create community platforms (networks, software) for the virtual plant enterprise
   b. Develop next generation toolbox of software and computing architectures for manufacturing decision-making
   c. Integrate human factors and decisions into plant optimization software and user interfaces
   d. Expand availability or energy decision tools (energy dashboards, automated data feedback systems, energy 'apps' for mobile devices) for multiple industry and diverse skill levels
2. Affordable industrial data collection and management systems
   a. Establish consistent, efficient data methods for all industries (data protocols and interfaces, communication standards)
   b. Develop robust data collection frameworks (sensors, data fusion, machine and user interface, data recording and retrieval tools)
3. Enterprise-wide integration: Business systems, manufacturing plants, and suppliers
   a. Optimize supply chain performance through common reporting and rating methods (dashboard reports, metrics, common data architecture and language)
   b. Develop open platform software and hardware to integrate and transfer data between small and medium enterprises and original equipment manufacturers (data sharing systems and standards, common reference architecture)
   c. Integrate products and manufacturing process models

(software network, virtual and real-time simulation, data transfer systems)
4. Education and training in smart manufacturing
   a. Enhance education and training to build workforce for smart manufacturing (training modules, design standards, learner interfaces)

Undoubtedly, there are complex challenges associated with creating access to cheaper standardized IT infrastructure platform for the manufacturing industries. However, benefits of technology driven adoption of cyber physical world within manufacturing realm is resulting in creation of new areas of innovation, increasing cost efficiencies, and driving sustainability. With unprecedented access to data coming from numerous sources, manufacturing is moving away from purely engineering driving innovation to data driven innovation. IOT based web of sensor technologies are driving collaboration among the cyber physical systems brining people, process, and data together, creating new business opportunities. Smart manufacturing is creating a truly connected enterprise. Insights from the production floors, business systems, essentially the entire supply chain interacts together, and optimize production and supply network. Manufacturing industries are quite diverse. On one hand of spectrum you would find manufacturing companies who are Research and Development (R&D) and Capital intensive, and on other end of the spectrum, you have manufacturing companies who are primarily labor intensive. Hence, the speed of digital technology adoption will vary from one type of manufacturing industry to another. Also, manufacturing industry will have to invest in elevating organization resource skill levels, and compete with other industries to retain digital technology experts. Digital technology will continue to facilitate new shape and structure to the manufacturing industry in the coming decade. Catering to customers' requirements for personalization, and tailoring to meet specific need across diverse markets is going to fundamentally change how next generation manufacturing creates value.

Smart Logistic
Logistic in simple terms is the process of moving goods from point of origin to point of consumption. However, within the various activities involved in the move process lies great amounts of variability, uncertainties, and complexities, impacting the bottom line of the business. Customers utilizing Omnichannels expects increased product customization, visibility on the stock levels, hassle free product return experience, shipment tracking notification, and are consistently demanding reduction in delivery time. This is forcing manufacturers, retailers, and logistic providers to find ultimate solution for global micro-delivery personal supply chain.

In order to holistically meet the micro-delivery demand with high levels of responsiveness, information transparency is needed to view both upstream customers' requirements, and downstream supplier's capability. Amazon owns the front-end customer relationship responsibility as well as the back-end logistic processes activities that encompass order management, inventory management, and order fulfilment. Amazon delivery fulfilment model manages link between their network of seller selling products, and the customers placing orders. Seller is responsible for shipping products to Amazon's one of the fulfilment centers, and thereafter product information gets loaded into Amazon's online system. The system receives and scans the product into inventory, record item storage dimension, and provide item label. The system then uses advance methods to locate the product, use high speed picking and sorting methods, and fulfills placed orders. This provides ability to both the seller and the customer to track their inventory and shipment. Utilizing technology and efficient processes, Amazon is able to successfully manage extreme market demand and supply volatility, and grow their ecommerce business.

Rise in technology is shaping the logistic industry. Let's look at some of the technology driving logistic innovation:

RFID

In the world of omnichannel and mobile devices, unlike traditional brick and mortar stores, online shoppers expect consistent visibility on stock availability. Capturing real-time inventory levels is a complex supply chain inventory management goal that every business endeavors to achieve.

Furthermore, gaining inventory visibility across omnichannel brings in other benefits, such as high order fill rate, low inventory storage cost, low margin loss due to markdowns, minimized inventory out of stock situation, and thus leads to a holistically efficient logistic process. Though, the problem complexity varies from business to business, inventory status across the supply chain network which includes distribution centers, physical stores, and in-transit inventory is highly dynamic and changes rapidly. This causes businesses a huge struggle to balance and optimize inventory to match customer demands without hurting the bottom line.

Somewhere around 2003, Walmart adapted the use of Radio-frequency identification (RFID) technology. Walmart pushed its partner suppliers to incorporate RFID in product and logistics process to gain item-level visibility throughout the supply chain. The biggest advantage of RFID is that unlike barcode it doesn't require line-of-sight to be read, and RFID tagged items can be read wirelessly in different orientation at a very high speed. Unfortunately, radio frequencies have limitations to pass through liquids and metal, and couldn't get the anticipated reliable read rate.

There has been since, several advancements in RFID technology, and various types of tags are now available for use in different environmental conditions. "Xerafy" who is a global provider of high quality industrial RFID, has pioneered RFID that not only offers full performance on and near metal, but also gets embedded within metal.

Embedded RFID seamlessly and invisibly gets integrated into the products at the time of manufacturing. Offering product that is either "RFID ready" or fully "RFID enabled" right at the point of manufacturing, enables a business to differentiate their product line from their competition. RFID enables item-level visibility, provides location and date-stamps of goods as it moves throughout the distribution process, allowing businesses to provide accurate information about the location of stock to customers as well track the progress of goods in transit. Studies have shown that enabling item level visibility using RFID technology could improves inventory accuracy from 65% to a staggering 95%.

A number of omnichannel retailers are looking up at RFID technologies to compete against online retailers like Amazon. US based omnichannel retailer "Macy" has successfully launched same day delivery services to 17 regions in US, and has attributed program success to high confidence in inventory accuracy as a result of RFID. Similarly, "Target" the Minneapolis-based American omnichannel retailer is working with its key vendors to outfit price tags with RFID smart labels sometimes by 2016 in its entire store to improve inventory accuracy, and out-of-stock issues. Target expects RFID to have an impact on its e-commerce operations, helping to fulfill online orders placed for store pickup, which amounts for 15 percent of Target sales, thus providing seamless experience between online and physical stores.

So far, Amazon has not used RFID, doesn't have planograms in its facility ,nor does it organize items by categories, and rather lets system guides items to be placed on the shelves that fit the size and maximize efficiencies.

Image Source: Getty Images

However, Amazon has now partnered up with RFID Lab at Auburn University. It is conducting a research into how RFID might be integrated into Amazon's existing software and robotics infrastructure at their fulfillment centers, focusing specially on tagging and driving inbound items through the fulfillment process. Amazon is in the early stage of exploring RFID, however believes the technology would further improves receipt of goods into the building, tracking of goods out to the customer, thereby further improving the customer experience.

Research from IDTechEx shows that in 2015, the total RFID market is worth $10.1 billion, up from $9.5 billion in 2014 and $8.8 billion in 2013. This includes tags, readers and software/services for RFID cards, labels, fobs and all other form factors, for both passive and active RFID. IDTechEx forecast that to rise to $13.2 billion in 2020. We will continue to witness evolution of RFID technology, its integration with other technologies and increased adoption by businesses.

Social Media
We previously discussed how social media and social networking are reforming how businesses are handling their interactions; connect with suppliers, customers, and even internal employees. Unfortunately, the logistics industry by large is slow in embracing social media strategies, despite many studies demonstrating that logistic leaders acknowledge the importance of doing so.

"Business Opportunities: Social Media 2013" paper lists opportunities that logistics companies could benefit from if they used the social media tools to build "expert collaborative communities".

1. Managing procurement and logistics using Social platforms, which allow instant communication between different parties on complex supply chains issues.
2. Improving organizational performance by streamlining communications and enhancing collaboration, both internally within the enterprise and outside with contractors, partners and suppliers.
3. Facilitating collaboration and co-creation, reducing the time spent in unnecessary in-person meetings, and helping share internal knowledge and best practices.
4. Accelerating the integration of new staff, contractors and outside partners into teams.

We are seeing the trend on how logistics companies have started adopting social media tools to form "expert collaborative communities". Smart Trucking has over 35 years plus experience in the trucking industry, and is using social media sites like Twitter, YouTube and Facebook to share information, advice, tips and other wide variety of information. Company's mission is to provide the other players in this business with the tools and skills they need for ongoing success.

Image Source: youtube.com/user/SmartTrucking

As logistic industry changes their misconceptions and stop quantifying the ROI on social media, we would see growth in logistics industry social media presence.

Mobile Technology

Traditional parcel delivery services and logistic companies are seeing an emergence of new package delivery business model based on mobile and cloud technology. Uber, a San Francisco based company focus on on-demand transportation services has expanded and extended their ridesharing model to a package delivery model. Uber has partnered with "Operator", the chat based shopping assistant, and started 1-hour delivery for "Operator" in

San Francisco area. Together they are competing against Amazon's massive warehouse advantage, by aggregating inventory for instant delivery from shops that are nearby. Currently over 100 of the most popular gifts from the Westfield San Francisco Centre mall, and Saks Fifth Avenue are available for immediate arrival. All shoppers have to do is to send "Operator" a plain text chat request for something they want, Operator finds and buys it for them, and an UberRush courier picks it up, and delivers it in an hour.

Uber with its innovative business model and technology is now disrupting the traditional logistics companies. Global shippers should always keep a close eye on technology that could disrupt logistics. Nevertheless, it'll be interesting to see what customers of the near-future will prefer, the personalized Uber delivery of a package, or the go-anywhere mechanical Amazon drone delivery which is the next topic of discussion.

Drones

Numerous innovations by Amazon have contributed significantly in bringing credibility to the e-commerce business, and there is no stoppage to that creativity flow. Amazon "Prime Air" is a future service that will deliver packages up to five pounds in 30 minutes or less using small drones covering a distance of 10 miles or more. These sophisticated drones using "sense and avoid" technology would fly under 400 feet and weighing less than 55 pounds. The company is working with US FAA (Federal Aviation Administration) for getting the necessary approvals.

Image Source: Amazon

Similarly, Wal-Mart Stores Inc has also applied to U.S. regulators for permission to test drones for home delivery, curbside pickup and checking warehouse inventories. Clearly, it is a sign that Wal-Mart plans to go head-to-head with Amazon in using drones to fill and deliver online orders. According to Walmart, drones have a lot of potential to further connect its vast network of stores, distribution centers, fulfillment centers and transportation fleet. There is a Walmart within five miles of 70 percent of the U.S. population, creating some unique and interesting possibilities for serving customers with drones.

Warehousing operation is going to see huge transformation as a result of drones. There won't be any unrestricted flight patterns within warehouse settings, and drones would be able to fly through the tight spaces, scanning every product in every shelf and becomes the future of warehouse inventory. Drone is no longer a farfetched idea, and it's going to transform both logistic transportation, and warehousing operation. More and more companies will embrace drone technology.

Augmented Reality

Wikipedia defines "Augmented Reality" (AR) as a live direct or indirect view of a physical, real-world environment whose elements are augmented (or supplemented) by computer-generated sensory input such as sound, video, graphics or GPS data. Augmented Reality or AR is causing a new wave of change in the logistic industry enabling faster, safer and smarter workflows. Research from Digi-Capital estimates the Augmented Reality market size to be around $120B by year 2020.

DHL in cooperation with their customer Ricoh and wearable computing expert Ubimax has successfully carried out a pilot project testing smart glasses and augmented reality for vision picking in warehousing operations in the Netherlands. DHL asked 10 of its warehouse staff to test various forms of augmented reality gear, such as Google Glass and VuzixM100, over a period of three weeks. The headsets were used to guide the workers through the warehouse, and identify items to be pulled – a method called "vision picking" – via a digital graphics on the smart glass. To the order picker, the units displayed task information, such as aisle number, product location and quantity of order, as if it were floating in the air before them. Order pickers picked up more than 20,000 items, fulfilling 9,000 orders within the given time frame.

INDUSTRY 4.0 DATA ANALYTICS

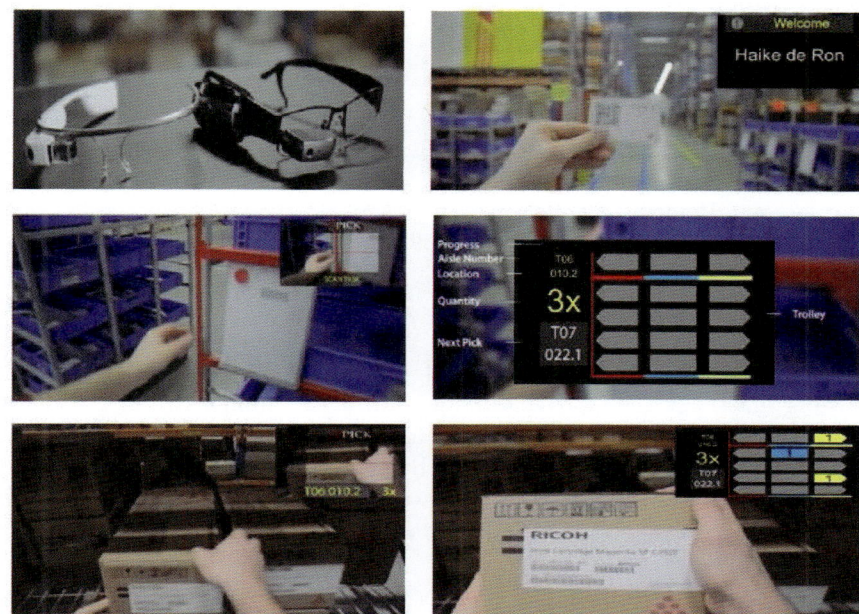

Image Source: DHL

Vision picking enables hands free order picking, thus greatly increasing productivity. The pilot showed a 25% efficiency gain with vision picking over traditional pick-by-paper approach.

AR ability to provide quick access to anticipatory information anytime and anywhere offers a huge potential for AR to play part in various other aspects of logistics value chain. AR adoption will continue to grow with more logistic providers embracing the technology.

IoT, Big Data and Analytics
Logistic industry is not new in terms of working with data. However, till now most players in the industry were performing basic analytics using generic business intelligence (BI) tools on the structured data.

Internet of Things (IoT) and Big Data Analytics are currently the most talked about trends within all industry segments including Logistics. Both IoT and Big Data analytics are creating agile and informed logistic network, driving increased productivity.

We talked in the previous sections about the growing usage of high stream data coming from connected smart devices. Here are some examples of sources of logistic and supply chain that have the potential to generate new type of value for the industry:

1. Mobile devices
2. Telematics
3. Electronics on-board recorders
4. Point of sale information and forecasts
5. ERP
6. RFID tags
7. Smart sensors
8. Web-based platforms

Big data analytics provides value through mining massive sources of structured and unstructured data, finding patterns and uncovering previously unknown relationships. The figure below captures the essence how the value from big data insight goes up as organization moves from descriptive, predictive, prescriptive to cognitive stage.

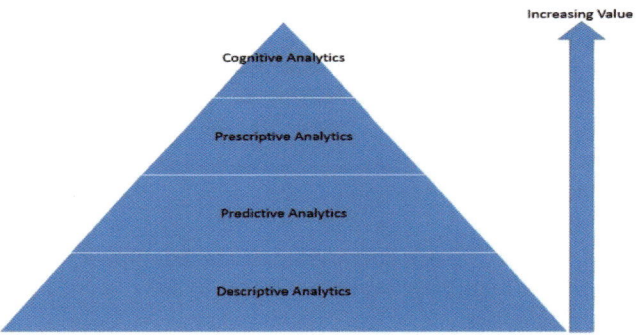

The followings section will describe some of the use cases wherein IoT and big data are already driving efficiencies within the logistics organization.

In-Transit Visibility through IoT and Data Analytics
Providing holistic in-transit visibility is one of the important application within logistic wherein IoT and big data has made significant inroad.

 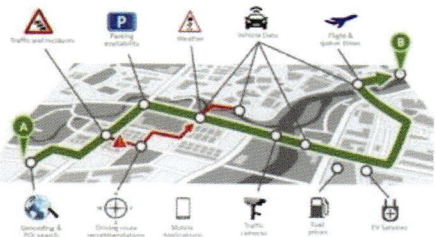

In smart fleets, transportation vehicles, packaging pallets and drivers, are all wired up with various sensors, thereby facilitating intelligence in the process. There are on-board diagnostic tools that are steadily collecting data from connected sensors and analyzing vehicle maintenance health status. Systems are able to predict when a critical part of the vehicle is going to fail, finds and book the appointment with the closest dealer shop in the route and notifies the driver about the appointment.

Performance data such as fuel consumption, idle time, rapid acceleration/ deceleration, over speed, distance travel is provided through telematics or mobile devices. This is crucial information for the company to perform analysis around mpg (miles per gallon) score, analyze driving behavior of drivers in the fleet and rate them against the fellow drivers. Furthermore, companies use the data to train the drivers and plan the corrective actions to improve driver scorecard.

Drivers are provided with wearable sensors that monitors parameters such as heart rate, body temperature, and stress levels. Hence, predictive analysis on the performance data coupled with the data coming off driver wearable devices is able to raise a red flag on the drivers more likely to cause accidents as a result of aggressive driving. This is helping companies to control risk and exposure through timely driver intervention. Hence, predictive modeling tools are providing companies opportunities for timely driver remediation, and are able to improve driver retention rate. This is extremely important as driver shortage happens to be most prominent issue in the transportation business. Similarly, sensors attached to the packaging are generating data such as weight, environmental temperature, humidity levels and product expiration date. This information in cases like perishable food industry is used to monitor the product in-transit quality.

Apart from the location data coming from vehicle, stream of environmental data such as traffic situation and weather forecast are on continuous basis fed from the cloud. Using predictive and prescriptive analytics, deliveries routes are re-routed. Furthermore, the data is used to estimate delivery times that is then relayed to the customer in real time, helping receiving department to schedule resources accordingly.

Conclusion

Logistics, a key facilitator in driving trade and economics, is undergoing transformation amidst technological advances. Since, global e-commerce adoption is growing at an exponential rate, there is pressure for enhanced agile B2B and B2C logistics services. Pace of technological adoption within logistic industry is gradually picking up the steam as logistic industry is working to overcome technological challenges similar to those seen in smart manufacturing.

IoT and big data technologies are enabling logistic companies to capture previously untapped unstructured data. There is a high volume of data coming from sensors, wearable devices, and other similar devices found on shipping containers, palettes, trucks, and planes. As well, data related to weather, traffic etc. from external environments is now available to be exploited.

However, traditional processes and systems are not designed to handle either high streams of data or unstructured data. Also, the logistic industry is facing integration challenges due to the lack of IoT device protocol and interface standardization which deters them to take full advantage of growth in IoT technologies. Nevertheless, there is enormous motivation to innovate, and numerous technological tools are continuously being tested and adopted. These innovations and automation in logistic processes are reducing cost, improving productivity, and generating data that creates further optimization opportunities. New logistic analytics software applications are powered by real time geographical location data, transportation cost estimators, optimization models and scenario managers that allow systematic evaluation and modelling of logistic networks and can thus recommend alternatives.

Next we are going to review how organizations are streamlining their organization structures to deal with digitalization and striving to stay relevant in the market place.

Emergence of new Digital Organization Structure

A digital organization is an enterprise that is in the forefront of exploring and selectively adopting the use of newer digital technology holistically across its ecosystem to create differentiation and gain competitive advantage in the market place.

The elements of a digital transformation

In the previous sections, we reviewed how the advancement and incorporation of Information Technology (IT) within organizations is shaking up the traditional processes and helping transforming businesses. Of course, the pace and the magnitude of digital transformation varies from business to business.

In order for businesses to succeed in their quest for digital transformation, they need a strong leadership that will drive the transformation through active engagement and governance. Companies' senior executives begin with crafting the digital vision and strategies. They evaluate various existing key business activities, scouting out the ones with the most potential to impact business results. The evaluation is done through building and using digital transformation suitability scorecard metrics to assess how various existing business processes and applications are rated. It's important to understand that in order for digital transformation to be effective, the transformation has to address end to end business processes, break silos, and foster collaboration.

The most common areas where companies look for digital transformation opportunities, are customer experience, operational function and the business model.

To begin, the customer experience is one of the most crucial factors in determining a customer's loyalty, and it is quintessential that this area be as optimized as possible. In an omnichannel environment providing customers a seamless integrated experience should be one of the key focus digital transformation areas, and some of the questions all companies should be constantly evaluating their status quo processes on are:

1. What needs to be improved in the existing customer touch point processes?
2. Which analytical tools will help to gain an understanding about the true needs and concerns of the customers?
3. What technology will help enhance customer experience and foster good relationships with the growing number of tech savvy consumers?

Similarly, various internal facing operational functions within companies could reap the rewards of going digital. Once again, companies must holistically review across the organization and evaluate gaps in the current digital foot-print. They should be asking:

1. What opportunities for work flow digitalization are not currently being exploited?
2. What are the current routine tasks or transactions that can be automated to shift employees focus from repetitive work to innovation?
3. How can digital collaborative tools and technologies elevate and foster cross-functional collaboration, and thus improve employee engagement in a geographically dispersed workforce?
4. What new capabilities and mind-sets are needed to support execution and sustainment of digital strategies within the company?

On the business model front, companies should consistently evaluate how they are providing digital offerings to the customers. Keeping in mind that technology is just an enabler and not the end goal, digital teams should passionately understand every customer touch-point through a human lens; how it operates, frequency of touch points, what devices are used, and how it can be further optimized and automated.

Once the strategy blueprint is ready, companies can start to design final digital strategy for executing new technologies and experiences. However, the biggest common challenge most companies face is how to create focused digital team structure that not just discover opportunities and drive digital transformation, but also are able to drive cultural transformation, which is the key for sustaining a successful digital organization.

There is no one model that fits all, however primarily one of four different models are common to find within the companies to manage and govern the digital team structure. Jason Mogus, Michael Silberman, & Christopher Roy on Stanford Social Innovation Review (SSIR.ORG) referred them as informal, centralized, independent, and hybrid. Here are how these four models look like:

Informal

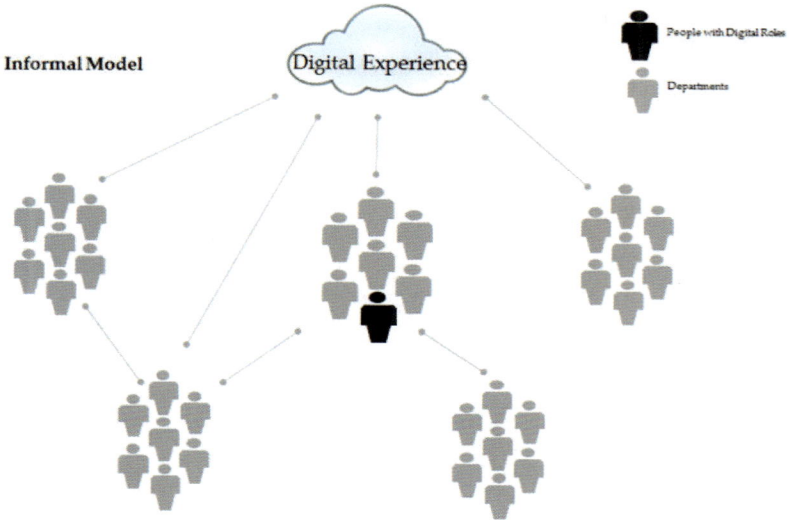

In this structure, program funding drive the needs, and digital work is loosely dispersed across various functions and departments. This is quite an inconsistent structure that lacks brand consistency, and yet surprisingly some organizations are stuck with it.

Centralized

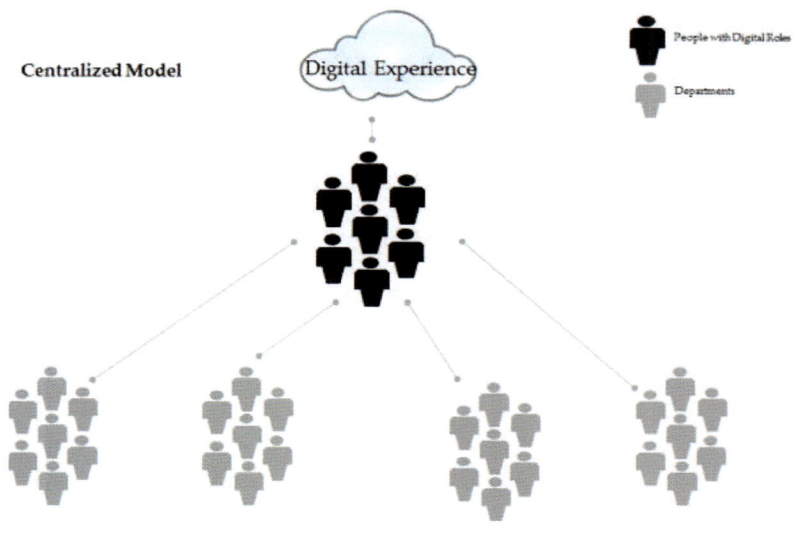

Here, the goal is to create a focused central function that provides consistent messaging, common tools, and clear roles and responsibilities. In this structure, the digital team members have strong technical and publishing skills, however lack the ability to provide content leadership, design and engagement with other teams. As a result, digital team members often get bogged down in heavy process that stifles their creativity.

Independent

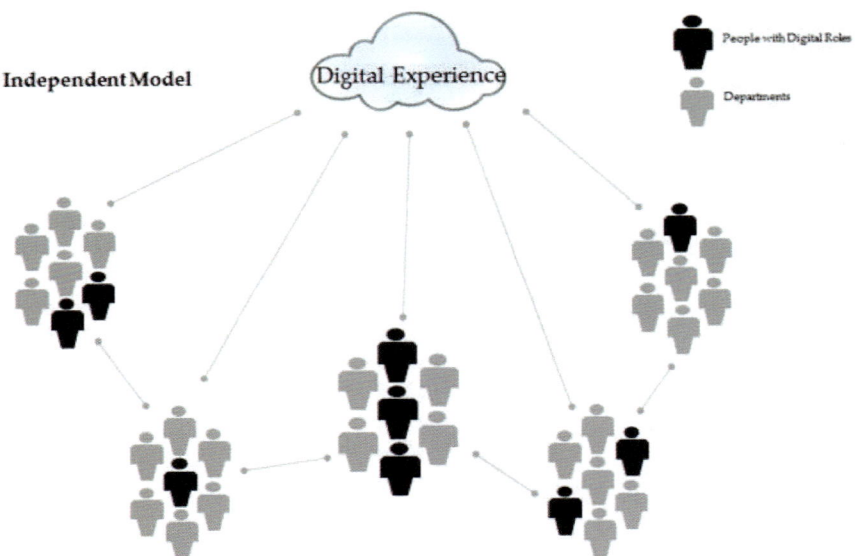

In this model, multiple centers of digital leadership are created across the organization. Unfortunately, this creates silos in which there will be some departments with a high performing digital culture which is isolated from the rest of the institutions. On other hand, there will be some departments struggling with under-resourced digital teams. This model often fosters a competitive rather than collaborative culture as no one looks holistically end to end.

Hybrid

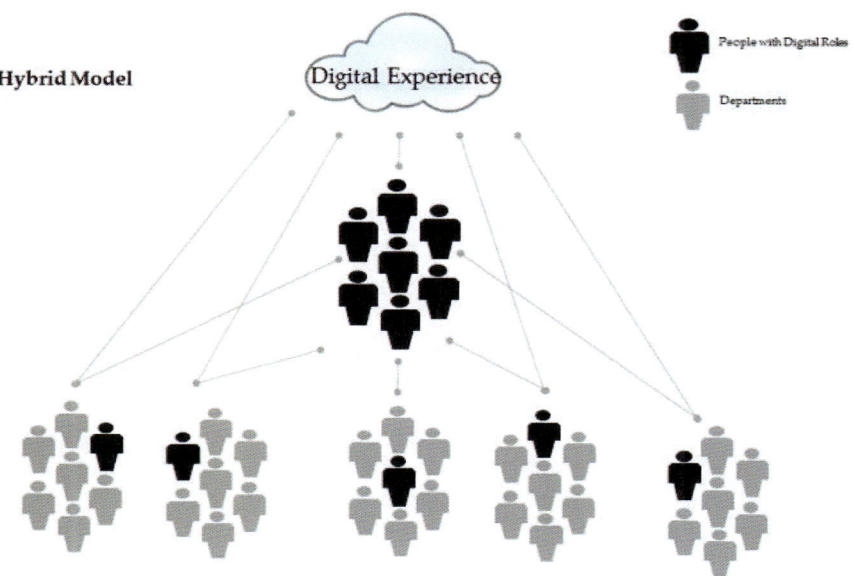

This is the most progressive and conducive model to produce continuous digital innovation. In this model, each different business function is supported by digital staff based on the needs. The digital staffers themselves are connected and supported by a central and strong experience digital teams that aligns and push the entire system towards the long term goal. This creates hyper connected teams and fosters highly collaborative culture.

How companies would want to create the digital organization structure and push the wheel of transformation is an important decision. Along with setting the digital structure, there are other elements that needs planning and attention. Employee education plays an important role, however it is not sufficient alone. Digital team members have to do heavy lifting, and passionately champion the digital transformation journey. Consistently, members have to instill the overarching goal and share what needs to be done and how. It's important to make every employee a cog in the wheel and have their "skin in the game" for digital transformation to work across the organization.

Digital transformation is a journey for a company to fundamentally realign their business model, their technology, and their processes for delivering customer experience, by effectively engaging with the evolving digital consumer throughout the consumer experience lifecycle. It's about reimagining the entire journey, and ensuring your business stays relevant in the digital era.

Data Analytic as new Function

Though, traditional businesses are data driven, however they lack the ability to provide faster response time that is needed in making business decisions every single day. Usually, the data analytic team members consist of SaaS, SPSS, deep statistical modelling professionals who are silo in their roles and expertise. Also, companies usually have a rigid IT department prioritization request process, wherein any new request to create reports or certain data have to joins the long prioritization queue. However, this approach will not work in the new digital economy, where business leaders are under immense time pressure to make decisions. Business partners and leaders can't afford to have their request for data insight goes through the IT priority queue, and then through the development and latter comes out after 3 months when no one needs it anymore. Since, business partners and leaders can't afford to wait, in the absence of prompt support they usually follow themselves a hard way to get closer to what they need to make decisions. They will continue to make decisions irrespective if data analysts are able to provide timely insights or not. Delivering a data insight 70% accurate tomorrow is considered better than delivering 100% accurate in a 3 weeks' time when it loses its relevance. The need is to make most informed decision in the shortest amount of time. Hence, IT needs to move faster than the business does.

There is a paradigm shift in the skill set needed for data analytic team members. Deep statistical modelling is mainly needed if you are building next generation of analytical tools. However, most businesses today need people with a broad spectrum of skills such as business skills, ability to relate to business partners, access and analyze data, though not necessary provide a perfect solution but enables a solution that they can communicate in business terms to make a decision. Also, soft skills are more critical and much needed. There is quite a bit of overlap and shift from traditional analytics role from IT to business side. Team members in data analytical teams have diverse background, and it's now common to see hard-core IT programmer, BI professional, Traditional business analyst and data visualization professional coming together with the willingness to learn business knowledge, and have the curiosity to discover and solve business problems. They don't just accept a number and rather peel the onion to find what is driving that number, what's behind it.

Accelerated business pace is pushing business partners and leaders to enhance their own data analytics skills, enabling them to integrate analytics in their day to day work to gain quality insight. This has triggered the new requirement wherein business partners demand access to data and tools themselves to analyze and gain insight. One of the new role of data analysts is to facilitate providing tools and technologies in the hands of business partners. However, often business partners will pick and choose numbers that will make them look good. Thus, business analysts must build relationships with partners and have a seat on the table with them to develop the best practices, educate them on the right way to analyze data, and create consistencies or one version of the truth. Deploying interactive dashboards over portal through blending analytics and visualization tools helps C-level and upper level executives improve their insight, enhance their understanding and appreciation for data. It's also critical for the data analytical team to build good relations with IT teams as IT owns the data and its architecture and helps the analyst to consume data and gets insight.

Companies who perceive themselves as more successful than their competitors, attribute their success to their ability to integrate data insights into the executive decisions making process. They are sophisticated in their use of data, use more sophisticated tools such as predictive analysis, prescriptive analysis, sentiment analysis and data visualization on a regular basis. Also, they have both the ability to perform real-time analytics on large complex data sets, and act on the outcome on a nearly real time basis.

Building a Successful Data Analytic Culture

Data analytics is the most critical spoke in the digital wheel of disruption. Companies must develop strategies to embrace the culture of data analytics.

IBM Institute of Business Value published a result from a study that identified nine levers to distinguish leaders who are able to realize value from big data and analytics from those who don't. Further, they group the nine levers into a progression of three steps; Enable, Drive and Amplify.

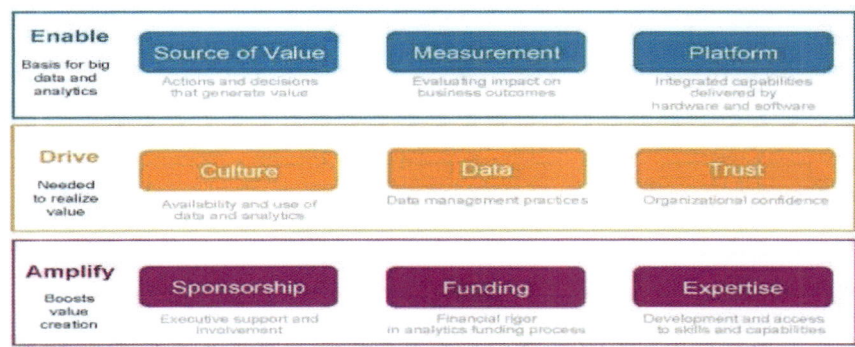

Enable consist of actions and activities that forms the foundation for creating value, measuring outcomes and providing platform for big data and analytics activities.

Drive consist of actions that are needed to create value from moving analytics discovery to value creation, which is aided by having an analytics and big data culture, data governance and security and creates trust.

Amplify increases the amount of value realized by providing momentum to translate insights into action that increases organization's bottom line. This is done through sharing a common vision, managing and monitoring analytic investments, and knowledge-sharing opportunities.

In the subsequent chapter, we are going to build on the above high level described framework for fostering a data analytic culture.

In conclusion, data analytics is more than a tool or a technology. It is a driver that culturally transforms the decision making discipline of the business. We truly believe that today's business will succeed only if they master the application of analytics to all forms of data. There is no industry where data analytics cannot make a positive impact.

CHAPTER FOUR

SETTING AN ANALYTICS CULTURE

"Speaking the same language..."

Changing an organization's culture starts from the top. Senior leaders need to see the value of their investments and incorporate it into the organization's key priorities. Setting up an analytics culture requires similar alignment from the top. Leaders need to start using data and facts to make decisions and investments for data acquisition, and data warehousing technologies and analytics focused teams need to be in place to lay the foundation for generating data driven insights.

Marcus is a supply chain director for a MNC. When he was first identified for the role, his challenge was with product availability escalation from regional partners every quarter end. People were having conferences almost every other night, going over customer orders, figuring out product allocation and distribution alternatives. Air expedite was a norm at the end of every end.

However, Marcus had an idea, and he believed that through systematic data analytics the root causes of the problem could be identified and the supply chain could be optimized. He started getting an analytics team in place to study the root causes, review safety stock level and redefine the business process. Three years later, air expedite was reduced by half, customers were more than happy with the service level they were getting, and even sent a personal thank-you notes to the accounts team. Three years was a long journey for Marcus. Setting up an analytical culture and getting people to embrace it did not happen overnight; but eventually it paid off.

Why are we sharing this case study with you? Embedding analytics within a company's DNA requires behavioral adjustments that may take a considerable amount of time and need consistent attention and focus. It's an exciting yet taxing journey that requires support from all angles, whether financially, or as a company success metric. As shown below, companies who successfully implemented an analytics culture are reaping the benefits of their investment. Analytics forms the basis of effective utilization of data and generates insights that are not just limited to helping companies define a strategic direction to take or sales strategies, but also aid in reducing costs.

Image Source: Information week

Next we are going to cover how a proper analytics team is structured, what tools are available, and review some important supply chain analyses that can be made. Many companies and organizations have either already established an analytics culture, or are in the process of setting one up. Regardless of where you are in the journey, we hope in the following chapters we will be able to provide you with the practical information and case studies that will lead you and your company into your own analytics success story. We have taken several case studies and discussion points from real world analytics implementation and have highlighted some common problems. By sharing this knowledge, we hope it will give you a head start into your own analytics journey.

Analytics Team Member Structure

When a company needs to setup a team for an analytics study, they can either look for people from within the company itself or hire external consultants for the job. An external consultant will have the relevant expertise for what the study requires, which in turn gives companies a fast turnaround of results. Consultants are experienced, having worked with many other companies in similar industries and hence in one way, the study outcome results are attested with high degree of confidence.

Analytics not only requires hard data skills, but demands a strong business knowledge, which people from within the organization possess for the task. Undoubtedly, developing one's own talents for the analytical job takes a much longer time, but in the long run, it will reap high returns against the effort spent. Therefore a company should also consider building their internal analytics resource capabilities which is also a cheaper option in the long run than hiring consultants.

There are different ways to organize an analytics team. Certain companies prefer to set up a dedicated analytics team which is a common resource for everyone across the company. Another method, is to have each function setup its own analytics team who specializes in the subject matter of studies. The first method definitely provides a better cost structure, but it also means the resources will be more thinly spread. Having your own focused analytics team within your function will typically yield better result since the same people are the domain experts at the same time. Domain experts play a very important role in identifying hypothesis and validating business processes. Hiring a data scientist without business knowledge is as good as a hiring a novice sailor to steer a ship through treacherous waters he has never traversed before; it will be a bumpy, disorganized ride that would not leave the ship or its passengers on board in a very good shape at the end. A dedicated team will also have a more focused effort and thus will be able to produce analysis in greater depth than a single, companywide analytics team trying to serve the needs of all the departments, and will be constantly battling amidst thin bandwidth.

Analytics success is typically achieved through a group of people who have different skillsets required for the analysis. Overall, the team possesses an in depth understanding of the business processes, advanced statistical knowledge, and proficiency in the usage of various analytics tools.

Here is a breakdown on the team structure and responsibilities for each role:-

i. Business Analyst
ii. Data Expert
iii. Data Scientist
iv. SMEs

Business Analyst
A business analyst plays the role of a catalyst in leading the analytic discussion by asking business questions and deriving results toward improving the business metric. They are well acquainted with the problems, business process and the strategy of the organization, and will be the one initiating different kinds of analysis. When data science becomes a challenge to be understood by stakeholders, business analysts can also act as a bridge between the data scientist and the stakeholders.

Stakeholders have a business focus and pain point that they are trying to alleviate or resolve, and they might want the solution in a certain format which they perceive is correct. In one of our discussion with a senior management team, we were asked to come up with a data modeling tool that could predict the transit time impact due to various factors. While discussing, we realized that there was an intention to keep random failure mode (such as truck failures) as an input to the prediction model. It is possible, but our question was when do you know a truck breakdown will happen? What the senior management really wanted was a model that could enable them to anticipate delays in shipments. The business analyst understood this as a requirement and proposed to simulate the delays as a probability rather than being designed as an logical input factor.

The business analyst also plays the important role of orchestrating the data analysis, from identifying the project scope, setting the right data preparation scope, and most importantly, providing the team with business objectives and possible business hypotheses to start the analysis.

Data expert
A data expert will be someone in your organization who might be system savvy and knows how and where to get the required information. People usually see data gathering as a simple downloading process, however this view is incorrect. Preparing the right data starts from first defining what are the crucial parameters, deciding the data period, and involves much more than just collecting the data. Data required for the analysis needs to be formatted into the desired rows and columns, and most importantly, validated for accuracy. The data preparation process is truly crucial to the accuracy of the final result, and data experts are the ones you need to help lay a robust foundation. Preparation of data usually uses up more time than what people expect, but there is no short cut to that. If you are planning any analytics projects, be sure to set away more time for data preparation.

Data scientist
Data scientists takes organized data, and perform modeling and data studies to look for clues and create insights. While data scientists are purely focused on the back end analysis job, in some organizations, they can be extremely influential if they happen to possess business knowledge for that analysis. Data analysis is quite exploratory in nature; you usually end up with more findings than what you initially set out for. In that essence, when collecting data, we usually try to keep the data to manageable size but also include any other data we might need, just to avoid missing some. A data scientist will be looking for all sorts of correlations and patterns by using the available data. Knowing how the business operates will help data scientists slice and dice data into smaller groups for further observations.

SMEs

The best people who have the authority on and truly understand the parts of the business are the subject matter experts (SME). There are many reasons why SMEs should be heavily involved in the analytics project. SMEs runs daily operations and have a vast experience in the issues and challenges they faced every day, so much so, that they will be a good source of input when looking for business issues and causes. Getting the SMEs involved in the process also means they can have a stake in the process and thus own the findings and contribute to implementing solutions. As well, SMEs are good sources of data cleansing inputs, especially when the data quality is not perfect. Stakeholders always rely on their SMEs to validate the accuracy of analysis and hence it is crucial to make them part of the team.

Tools

Often, people can get quite obsessed with the tool selection when it comes to setting up an analytic culture in the organization. Contrary to many beliefs, you do not need to have access to expensive modeling tools to be able to perform good data analysis. People who get overly obsessed with tools often find out that the complexity and cost becomes a burden to the organization. Modeling and simulation software often requires well trained users and typically pose an issue when these experts leave the organization. Each tool has its strengths and weaknesses, and so it is important to choose the right tool for the purpose and not go beyond what is needed. In practice, most supply chain data analysis does not involve simulation or even complex statistical functions.

One of the most used tools is Microsoft Excel. Excel has evolved over time from a simple spreadsheet to pivot tables, and there is plethora of available plugins that offer all sorts of advanced statistical analysis. If you are well versed in supply chain process flow and logic, you can actually build logics into Excel and start your own supply chain simulation.

Additionally, there are also many data visualization tools being offered in the market. Data visualization tools offer both simplicity in grouping data and ease of database connectivity. Most tools offer capabilities in managing bigger datasets than Excel can manage, which is an important consideration in choosing the tool. Templates and dashboards can be created, and for beginners, you have the choice of trying from an array of charts to represent the data. More and more organizations are adopting visualization tools since the outputs are more easily understood and adopted by people who are less acquainted with databases. Reports can be linked to different forms of databases and you get a refresh of the data quite conveniently.

Excel and data visualization tools offer qualitative analysis. Without third party Add-Ins, there are limitations to the analysis when it comes to quantitative studies. There are however dedicated statistical software packages that offer not only statistical analysis, but also correlation studies, design of experiment, and simulation options. Examples of such tools are Minitab, JMP, and R. Tool choices are pretty much associated with the exposure the users has when they first started analytics. Certain users prefer more customization and software coding ability that gives them more options and flexibility with their analytical study, such as R. A different camp of users may find JMP easier to start with. Therefore it is mainly a choice dependent on the analytical needs and how proficiently one can use the software.

Whether you are using Excel or any other Data visualization tool, the fundamentals of data analysis does not change. Tools should not be viewed as enablers for analytics. Being overly obsessive about the tools can only burden the company and rather it is important to focus on being efficient in using what is needed for the job and learning to use it to its full potential. It will be not realistic to expect a novice photographer to produce masterpiece by simply passing him a professional camera. Having a good tool with the latest technology gives you a head start, but the fundamentals of how data should be composed and a practiced patience for details are what makes a good data analyst.

However, it is imperative to choose the right tool for the scope of the study involved. You might have to use different tools at different stages of the project. We usually start with Excel for arranging and cleaning up data, visual tools for hypothesis and observation, and eventually one of the statistical packages for model building. Excel is pretty handy in most aspects of the problems we study. In latter sections, few of the case studies and simulation that you will read were all modeled using Excel.

Data resource

Data availabilities are the pre-requisite before you can even start any analysis. In all the data analysis projects we have worked on, the most time consuming and challenging part is to get hold off the right data set. Data is usually not easily available, not tracked nor organized, or requires experts to access. In large companies, data is usually available through ERP software whereas in smaller firms, this may be available largely through manual tracking.

Certain data, even though available, is not available in the granularity required by the data studies. Certain details might be good to have, however analysis shouldn't bottle down because the data is not perfect. We always work around the situation by first understanding how critical the data constraint to the end result is. Many analysis results are often used to set investment directions and thus if the outcome shows a significant difference in savings, precision in this case would not change the story anyway.

Data integrity, on the other hand, does pose a problem to analysis. Often the data is organized in different databases especially when data is manually tracked. In such cases, the collected data might show incorrect information which is totally off the grid or even a wrong match. Imagine messing up the carrier names while studying carrier contribution to transport delays. This is quite different from the accuracy problem we discussed earlier, and can lead to total different findings. Safety checks need to be in place to screen or prevent data issues, and should include using other data sources or information as a triangulation check; SMEs are good source of data validation as well. Do cater in more time during project planning if this is the first time the data is collected. Experience shows that it can take more than 50% of the total project duration just to get the data collected and validated.

Different types of data analytics

Data analysis is used quite generally and broadly by people when their work involves the manipulation of spreadsheets and numbers. Can we consider all works involving data as an analysis? And how much of the data analysis is actually providing valuable insights to your organization? Often people tend to mix reports and analytics together. We will get to the difference between the two later, however the point we are trying to highlight here is that if you are not aware of the differences, you are probably not reaping the benefits of analytics. Yes, all the work we are doing should bring new intelligence for decision making otherwise we are not maximizing our investment in analytics. In the following topics, we are going to categorize data analysis into different sections, so that it is easier to understand what kind of works, tools and resources are needed. Different analysis requires different forms of training and competency, so it is critical to match the man to the job requirement.

Business Reports
Reports are the most common form of data analysis people create or use every day. Reports in general takes less time and templates are usually created so the data is refreshed to provide trends and alerts. Reporting is a process of transforming data into information to indicate performance level and status. Reports are the first level of information for stakeholders and it serves as an alarm to measure the effectiveness of everyday operations. An example of a report is the daily production report. A daily production report gives you

important information such as whether shipments are on time, how yields are performing, and production downtime. But while reports show symptoms they do not contain a deep level of insight such as what happened, where it happened, and most importantly, reports don't provide options for stakeholders. Data analysis involving insights are called Business analytics. Reports are a good form of control and monitoring mechanism but has a different purpose.

Business Analytics

Here is a scenario. The latest market share report showed the market share of your company has dropped 3% year on year. Your director has asked you for a detailed analysis on what led to that fall. Your data shows that the market decline started in summer. However, market share decline happens only for the European market. Further competitive analysis and market research reflects that the competitor has launched a new product during the same period. The smartphone product has a bigger display and its customer take up rate has gone up. Your latest analysis has helped the company review its new product strategy timely.

Adding insights to the available information helps businesses understand where improvements are much needed. Analytics involves a deeper dive of data answering who, what, where, when, why and how. While reports provide performance indicators, analytics provides ideas for improvements. It doesn't quite help if you hire a coach who merely tells you are not performing well, rather than suggesting ways to improve. A lot of business partners we worked with are not motivated to perform more analytics. They complain about being inundated with updating and maintaining various reports. Analytics does take up more bandwidth to allow deeper fact findings. It is crucial for any management trying to adopt an analytic culture to allow time for people to keep drilling for fine details and causes, rather than spending more time on just publishing reports. Once all the problems are systematically solved, people will start to have more bandwidth to do more insightful studies, and that is how you start nurturing the fruits of success and improving business fundamentals.

Predictive Analytics

What we have illustrated so far are examples of post event analysis. But the demand for analysis has shifted to a more proactive and predictive environment nowadays. Predictive inputs can come from historical knowledge or current intelligence from sensory inputs, in the form of structured or non-structured information. Structured data is better organized in categories and numbers, while un-structured data can be textual comments, images or even voice recordings. We derive information using such inputs, establish patterns, and predict the possibilities of the next occurrence of an event. If we have the knowledge of what is coming, when it is arrives, we will be better able to assess its magnitude of impact and be better prepared. Predictive model helps organizations mitigate or avoid potential risks and catastrophes from happening.

Predictive analysis requires resources that are well trained in statistics as it involves use of advanced statistical tools. Predictions can come as extensions of current data trends, through trend charting, or through machine learning of patterns. Predictive concepts are not used in just predicting events or trends. The development of data collection capabilities has since allowed online retailers to study customer profiles and purchase patterns, allowing them to use that information to further recommend products which might interest the customers. Credit card companies on the other hand, use customer profiles and credit history to associate and predict the chances of a customer defaulting. In supply chain, historical data is used with statistical algorithms to derive better forecast and predict order behavior. As you can see, predictive analyses are very powerful and allow you to act ahead of events and are a source of competitive advantage.

Simulation/ Prescriptive analytics/ Optimization

Prescriptive analytics are the final phase of analytics. With the guided knowledge from previous analytics and predictions, what should we do next? Knowing the market share decline is good, but being able to prescribe actions to address that decline is much more valuable information. Prescriptive analysis reviews what the required action should be, given the kind of situation you are or will be in. In order to quantify the potential choice points, prescriptive analysis is typically bundled with simulation so that one can model the potential outcome if certain actions were to be taken. This also allows optimization studies to determine the best operational conditions.

There are two categories of simulation: - Static and Dynamic. Static simulation runs simulations based on given rules and algorithms in the software. Given the required inputs, the software will produce a required set of computed output metrics. These metrics are what is important to the business, and being able to simulate the outcome is critical for leaders to understand the potential impacts of a choice they make. Time to market is important and so business decision needs to be screened and narrowed down to possible choice points without having to go through expensive and risky market trials and error. Simulation allows a quick studies of scenarios without the actual cost of implementation. As an example, supply chain analysts use such tool to study the inventory and the operational cost of their new network prior to making a hefty investment of capitals in setting up the physical distribution nodes.

Dynamic simulation software, on the other hand, models the time series behavior of a system with the intent of identifying and understanding the factors that control the system. Simulations run real-time, and take simulated inputs based on known historical distributions and intervals. Based on each pre-requisite condition, the model will run and produce the next state scenario, and this scenario becomes the input for the next run, and so the process continues. Dynamic simulations are extremely powerful in simulating and being able to record every single event, thereby allowing analysis into peaks and bottoms within minutes. As an example, banks use historical customer arrival rate to decide how many tellers should be open at the different time of the day ensuring queue time can be kept low but optimal according to the customer traffic flow. This helps banks to optimize their operation costs while ensuring customers do not spend too long in the queue waiting to be served. Dynamic simulations are used in other service sectors as well, such as planning traffic light timings and road capacity to ensure minimal congestion.

By now, you must have realized that simulation tools are a cost effective way for scenario studies and optimization. Once developed, a simulation model can run trials and scenarios almost instantly. Since everything runs on computers, risky events can be accessed without the need to run an actual physical trial.

Adopting simulation software however, has its own challenge. Other than the potential cost of owning the license, a simulation software does require a good amount of training due to its many complexities. The results can only be as accurate as the information given by the users, so having an experienced analyst is crucial, and talent retention becomes critical in this aspect. As discussed earlier, data availability is a very important pre-requisite for analytic studies. Simulation software forms the algorithm of a set of complex rules, and the rules run based on a set of required data which forms the pre-requisite to the whole analysis. In most cases, we do not have the luxury of data, especially when your organization has just started its analytics journey. In such cases, assumptions will have to be made or derived from the next closest existing data. A good example is when we were asked to determine the capacity and resource requirement in a manufacturing environment. One of the required input to the model was the equipment downtime patterns, but the only downtime being tracked were the time to repair for each event, and even that data was quite limited since the product only started running half a year ago. The limited downtime data was fitted to a Poisson distribution (since repair time typically follows long tail effects), and compared to other similar machines. In order to reduce the risk due to such estimations, we also created alternate scenarios for mean time to repair, so it shows the worst case story as well.

Simulation is a powerful technique, but as shown earlier there are possible calculated risks due to the amount and accuracy of data. Always practice triangulating your simulated result with actual performance, to test the validity of the model. Algorithms built-in modeling tools are theoretical in nature. Through actual practice, we have come to realize that most of the time, human behavior and emotions do impact the outcome, leading to cases where the end result can be quite different. When we were investigating the high amount of air transportation and inventory, we realized that half the time, the factory planners were shipping products through air and not adhering, but rather exceeding the safety stock target guidelines. The reason for this was that they foresaw more air shipments required in future demands, so they rationalized to ship more now. This was against the theoretical logic of shipping to recovery level, and something the simulation software wasn't able to predict. We were able to discover the problem because we triangulated the air shipments from simulated results against actual results, and that lead us into further investigation. When such situations occur, we cannot take the absolute results from the study. We typically recommend using the relative results between scenarios of studies to understand the relative gain and losses between different choice points. This also elevates the needs to be precise, depending on the modeling objectives.

Simulation can be done in any environment with or without the need for a commercially available simulation tools. We have customized numerous simulation studies by merely using Excel. These were non-standard studies that couldn't be done easily on standard simulation software. Algorithms were built inside Excel to emulate the behavior of supply chain process and best of all, we were able to customize and consider various human behaviors. You will find examples of some of the case studies at the later chapter when we discussed air shipments optimization.

Steps of Analytics

a. *Problem statement/ Business Objective*
When you start a project you want to be crystal clear on the expected outcome, intended use and the scope of the study. Project must come with clear measureable metrics on what is deemed as a success. Use scalable metric whenever possible, such as 10% reduction in air shipments. The problem at hand could involve a big scale data collection and so scoping the project well

help you keep the project duration to a manageable limit. Most complex projects are sized so that it can be completed within 3 months, you want to be time sensitive especially with data analytics. Long analytics projects might cause you to miss the boat to provide input for that important decision, or you may find that the information you used are no longer relevant. Using Pareto technique, we can reduce the scope within the biggest win area looking for the biggest return. Other approaches can also be where problems are more severe, or low hanging fruits identified through data visualization.

Invest some time and ensure the intended outcome of the project are clearly understood with the stakeholders as this will have an impact on what data, resources and tools are required e.g. Sensitivity study, root cause, predication model etc. This is when you also determine if the intended outcome is even possible, otherwise the project objective needs to be adjusted to fit the constraint.

b. *Hypothesis building (Using Qualitative Analysis)*

Back in 17th century, traditional fishermen had used trawling boat in search of fishes in the big wide ocean. As fish got scarce in the usual spot fishermen would start hunting for the next better ground for netting the fishes. This was the most effective ways of catching fishes then, but it could have been better, if only technology were more advance then. Modern fishermen scan the ocean using sonar, before laying down the nets. With the help of technology and studying the pattern of fish migration, modern fishermen are more effective and productive in narrowing down where to start hunting.

Data analytics is quite similar to the fishing; productive data analytics requires sufficient preparation to know where are the probable areas to start casting your nets. We achieve this through initial hypothesis building. Hypothesis building helps set us looking for evidences using initial clues we have, rather than spending time scouting the whole ocean.

Hypothesis traditionally comes from SMEs who are best familiar with the business, through interviews and brainstorming technique. Developments of visualization tools have enabled more efficient use of data itself as a hypothesis building source. Quantitative information can come from visual interpretation of the data collected, such as trends and groupings, spikes and bottoms. Searching for hypothesis within data can yield good returns, observations are usually found while quick scouting through the data. As hypothesis developed, you might have to reset your data criteria so that new information is added as part of the data collection requirements.

c. *Analysis method*

We need different tools and data for different form of data studies. Each analytics tool has its strength and limitation. Knowing what analysis is required and then choosing the right tools for the purpose of study is essential to maximize productivity. If the studies involve prediction model or multi-factors correlations you will need a statistical tool like JMP and R. If most of your works involves spreadsheets and statistics, Excel might be a better tool. In fact Excel is sufficient most time to perform scenario studies, sensitivity studies and single-factor correlation. Pivot table and charts in Excel also serves as good visual analytic tools. Dedicated visualization tools are also designed to provide better flexibility in database access and offer more options in chartings and performing dashboard reports. We use Excel most of the time as most of the tasks do not require complex modeling. In fact some complex modeling can even be performed in Excel. Once you understand the business and system process well, you can replicate the same logic in Excel and use it for simulation.

When the job requires more complex real-time or dynamic simulation, it is advisable to get specific simulation tools as well the associated expertise who knows how to code it. Different analysis will requires different level of expertise to be involved, the data required for certain simulation and statistical studies needs to be prepared and screened prior to the analysis. The important key here is to ensure that you plan ahead what is the desired output of your analysis, and deciding which tool and resources you will need, and ensure the data required is available.

d. Data collection and validation

Data forms the backbone to every analysis. Data can be from log sheets, surveys or even database archive. Additional time is needed to be factor in if data from log-sheets needs to be transferred into soft copy. It is always a good practice to decide ahead what data is required and how you want the data to be organized. Knowing that you needed additional data parameter at a later stage could cause a major setback in your analysis timeline, especially if the effort is to be done manually.

There are two typical extremes when it comes to deciding the data parameters, and the duration. When data is conveniently available, the project team may request for large data parameters for the longest duration it is available. However collecting large amount of data not only slow down the data collection process, it may also add burdens to the data checks resulting in slow down of the analysis. Depending on the analysis required, you might not want to mix older data with newer one, as older data might represent a totally different business or process environment. So going too far back in time might be counter-productive for the analysis.

The other extreme will be cutting down of data parameters and duration of data due to the complexity of data mining. In either case, we should not ask for more data merely if it is convenient, or undercut the information due to bandwidth limitations. There is no perfect answer, but we recommend some guidelines that you can do when deciding what parameters and data duration to use. As we mentioned in the earlier analytics steps, the team with SME should start off by stating the project objective and/or problem statements. Data choices need to be aligned to the type of analysis or problem on hand. Building initial hypothesis will help to identify an initial list of parameters and data duration to prove the hypotheses. If you are not able to rule out the need of particular data, keep it. This will be easier than asking the data team to re-collect the data at a later stage. It is also a good practice to ask for data in the most raw and granular format as it helps you segregate problems into smaller chunks and effectively helps to narrow problem into a smaller manageable area to look at.

e. *Data validation and methods*

Data integrity is critical and should be validate before you even begin your data analysis. Data inaccuracy will lead to time wasting investigation, and worse of all leads to wrong findings. Data integrity can be compromised during data entry, data archive or even data preparation for analytics.

When working on thousands and even millions of rows of data, it is impossible to check every single data for error. Below we will discuss some of the ways to address some commonly faced challenge during data collection and validation techniques.

Duplicate values

Duplicates data might happens when combining data from various data sources, there are also times values can be aggregated to reduce the number of rows. Excel provides feature to detect and delete duplicate data, but how would you deal if you have data like below?

Shipment Reference	Date	Quantity
SZ1234567	3-Jan-13	8600
SZ1234567	3-Jan-13	8600
SZ1234567	5-Feb-14	4000

You want to remove the duplicate Ship reference SZ1234567 which is in both row 1 and 2. In this case the same ship reference has been recycled and reuse in 5th Feb 2014. Using the default method of removing duplicate ship reference you will end up deleting the new entry but that's actually a new shipment. So here's how to overcome the challenge:-

Look for two or more column data fields, combine them and create another unique data (You can use Excel Concatenate function to achieve this). In the example above, we can combine Ship Reference and Date. This is how it looks:-

Shipment Reference	Date	Quantity	Concatenate
SZ1234567	3-Jan-13	8600	SZ123456741277
SZ1234567	3-Jan-13	8600	SZ123456741277
SZ1234567	5-Feb-14	4000	SZ123456741675

Now we managed to create a unique concatenate data for the shipment in 5th Feb 2014. Using this new column, we can then go ahead and delete the rest of the duplicates using standard Excel function e.g. row 2.

Missing data/ Entry issues
There are occasions wherein improper data collection or errors made in data entry resulted in missing data or value. For scalable data we can perform a sum check at the end of the column or row with problematic row or column revealing a sum of 0. Another check can be through the use of Stdev function in Excel. Stdev will shows 0 for data range with identical values. Therefore this method is good for checking any data values which should be different but are not. There are also occasions where missing data are random, in such case plotting a line chart should shows those irregularities (See graph below). You can notice right away that there is a data entry issue on 1/7/2015; the year was entered wrongly in the original data so there had been 365 additional days added to that data. Another error of missing data was spotted for 1/10/2015. Missing categorical data does not add values to the analysis unless the correct information can be retrieved by other means. Some people might use their best intelligence to fill in the correct categorical data, but do take note that wrong information can lead to totally different conclusion. If the missing data samples are small it might be worthwhile to consider excluding them.

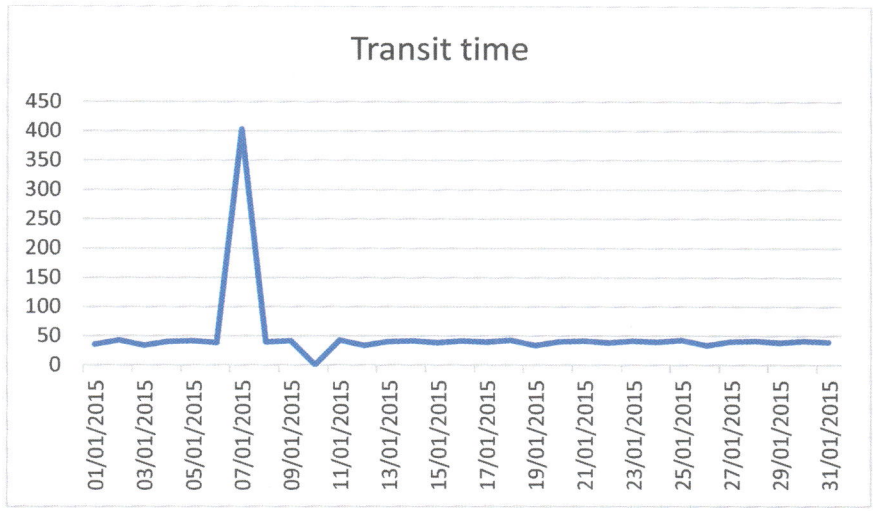

Sometimes the whole record of data can be lost during data pull or preparations. This can be crucial especially when data samples are limited. As much as possible validate and ensure available data is recovered and not lost in preparation. To check for missing rows or data count you will need information you can triangulate against, such as total number of participants, quarterly volume etc. You can also use Countif for checking number of valid records, or Sum function to validate aggregated volume in Excel.

Outlier (Entry error)
Outliers are common problem especially when data is manually entered. In other situations outliers may come from manual back tracking of information or cut and paste error during data collection. A good practice is always to use a Filter option and check the data range from the Filter drop-down list of values in Excel. Another visual method is to plot the values in a line chart and watch for spikes or dips in the data. You can also use Max or Min function to help you determine the extreme data values in a given range of data.

f. *Data Visualization*
What really makes data visualization so powerful? Data does not hold any meaning until it is deciphered. It holds no meaning until you arrange it in a manner that tells stories. Data visualization is an important stage in analytics wherein numbers and text are transformed and summarized into visual representation. Arranging data in the right manner using suitable graphical formats helps reveals important information hidden within the numbers. When use correctly it can show periodical events, trends, comparisons and

many other crucial evidences that will set the stage for next analytics path.

Humans do not work well with massive amount of data with information all over within millions of rows of data. Visual technique helps size that amount of information into a simple charts. We used colors, trends, categorizations etc. to highlight areas of opportunities and failures. Stacking transportation segments in column chart helps you understand both trends and proportion of different transport segments in a logistic delay situation. A Pareto chart will help you identify and solve the most significant delay. Visual comparison among different datasets is much easier than to look at numerical values. Putting the information side by side using column charts will assist greatly in spotting that difference than scanning the whole range of rows of data.

Acceptances for data visualization techniques have grown tremendously and there are plethora of commercial data visual visualization tools from companies like SAS, Tableau and Qlikview to choose from. The development of new tools creates more possibilities to work with bigger data sets and added charting capabilities.

We also uses observations from data visualization to develop new hypothesis. With new hypothesis identified, you may have to go back and expand your data to a longer time horizon, or even adding more data details for the observation noticed.

Learning to use the right charting to tell the right story is crucial. Here are some examples of data representation using visual charting:

Pie Chart (Proportion)

These are useful to show the proportion of each category in making up the total. The pie chart below is showing the proportion of parcel arriving on a weekend, by different shipping date. Parcel arriving on weekends will have to wait for next week to be delivered, meaning a longer wait by the customers. Using Pie chart, we were able to see that shipping the parcel on Monday and Tuesday had higher probabilities of reaching the destination on weekends. This information was useful to the stakeholders; in fact there were times that additional work hours were put in to make sure products could be shipped by the beginning of the week, this was adding cost to the operation. The rush did not benefits customers since the parcels still reached the customers the week after, along with the deliveries made on Wednesday. Simple pie chart has helped in avoiding the additional cost of expediting shipments for Monday and Tuesday.

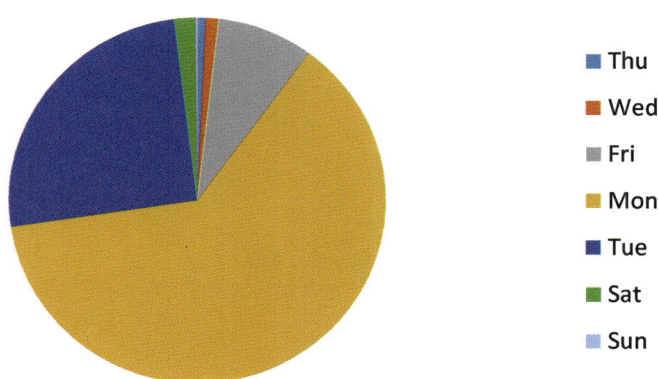

Pareto (Column chart)

The Pareto principles states that in general 80% of the effect you see are contributed by 20% of the causes. Pareto theory is commonly used to short list areas of opportunities by letting you prioritize and focus the limited resource on few key factors, yet solving 80% of the problems. Representing your information in Pareto is similar to Pie chart, except you first have to sort the data in descending orders, and further plot it into Column chart. Tackling the top few issues will help you maximize your returns.

You also have the option of adding the cumulative line. Cumulative lines help you visualize and estimates how much of the problem will be solved if the corresponding factors can be resolved. Using the previous examples again below, approximately 90% of weekends' delays can be avoided if parcels are shipped on Wednesday onwards.

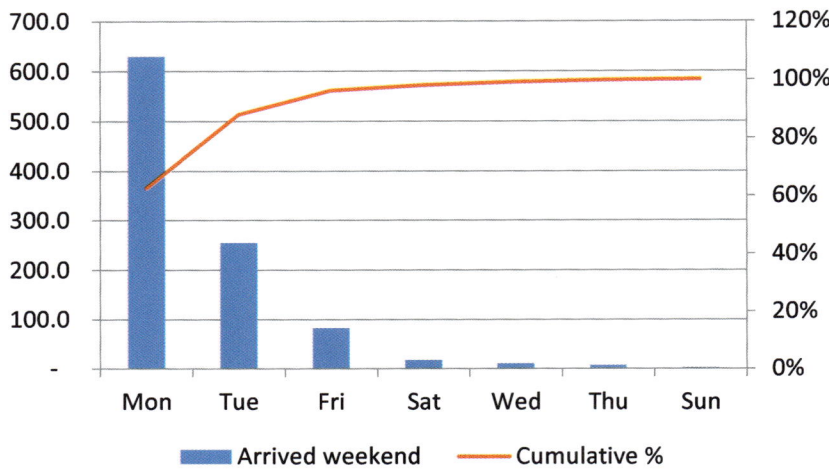

Trends / Line

Trend/ Line chart are usually associated with showing how scalable parameters perform over time. This is a useful technique in telling historical changes and highlighting event impacts. Below chart shows Port Labor negotiation event in West coast USA affecting the transit time of cargo beginning June 2014.

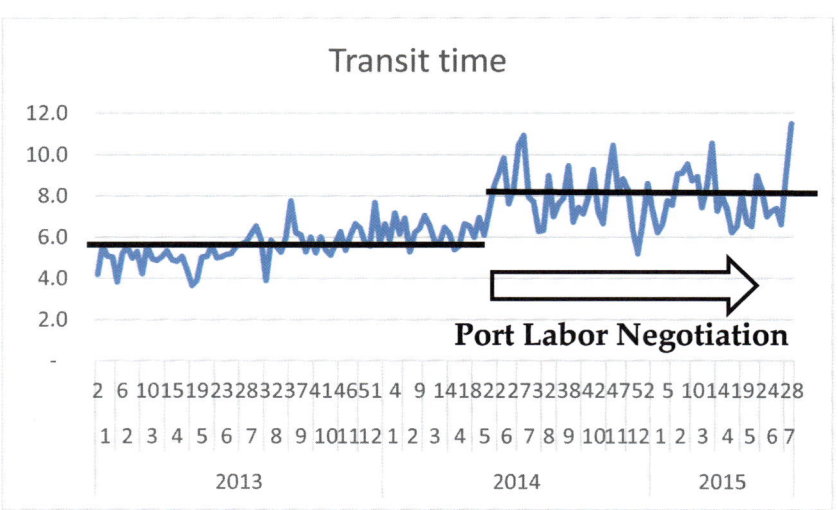

Line charts are also effectively used looking for recurring events. When you have data across a long time horizon, plotting the trend over time helps you spot the ups and downs and noticing patterns that are regularly repeating over a fixed interval of time. This technique is very useful especially when you are spotting correlation factors for predictive analysis. Sometime you might find that plotting each data as single point in the graph reveals too much random noise in the process and this might mask out the hidden patterns you were trying to find in the data. The random noise when observing single point data usually mask out some mid or long term effect on the process. To minimize the noise, we can aggregate and plot the average of few data points as one. As you increase the number of data aggregation you start to see the trend line smoothening out, and revealing more clearly mid and long term trend and shifts.

Data arranged in ascending time orders or counts are also used effectively to predict trends of a given process, when time or counters are an influencing factor e.g. Number of molded parts. Given the same operating conditions, mold life is closely associated to the numbers of molded parts. As more molded parts are produced, at some point abrasion will start causing the mold dimension to change resulting in produced parts failing dimensional specification. Parts specification failures could be avoided if we can predict the mold life. The relationship between the molded product dimension and numbers of mold shots can be best represented in this case by Scatter plots, which we are discussing next.

Scatter plot
Scatter plots are useful to show if there is a relationship between variables which can either be linear or non-linear. Data for one variable are plotted in the X axis and the corresponding value of the next variable is plotted in Y. The relationship can be measured by a correlation value that indicates how well the variables are associated to one another. Here is an example of the relationship between forecast error and demand volume. From the chart you can see forecast error (Coefficient Of Variance) is worst for low volume runners, since demands are more sporadic and less predictable. COV will be discussed latter in more details while discussing Safety stock setting. The relationship can be model closely through an exponential regression, with coefficient of determination 81% (R square). The fit is consider high (R square 81%, R=0.9) since R is >0.8. We can then use the regression to predict or estimate the corresponding COV given a particular demand.

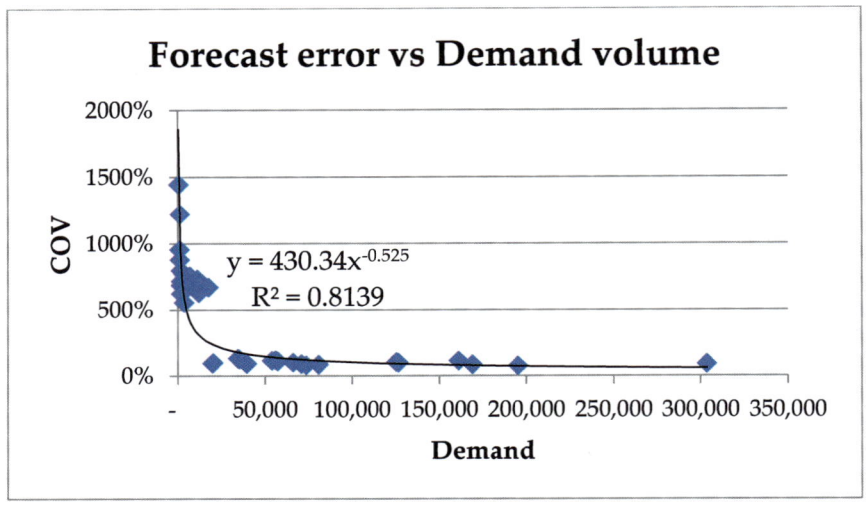

Histogram

Histogram is used to represent the distribution of numerical data. The Y axis represents the frequency of occurrences of a particular bucket of value or the probability distribution of the given data. Often people wonder if there is a difference between the Bar chart and histogram. Bar charts are used to display categories of grouped data wherein each bar represents one category and its associated values. While histogram is used with continuous data; the data is divided into bins (Representing a range of values) and plotted as what seems as a category. When performing statistical study you need to know how the data is distributed, whether you see a bi-modal, skew right / left, or normal distribution. The type of histogram can provide more clues for the data on hand. As an example, a bi-modal distribution might represent 2 separate grouping of performance, possibly a change or deviation in process, by 2 different carrier or even two different measurement gauges. You certainly want to split the grouping if there is. Here's a sample histogram for transit time, in this case the data is normally distributed averaging around 4 days.

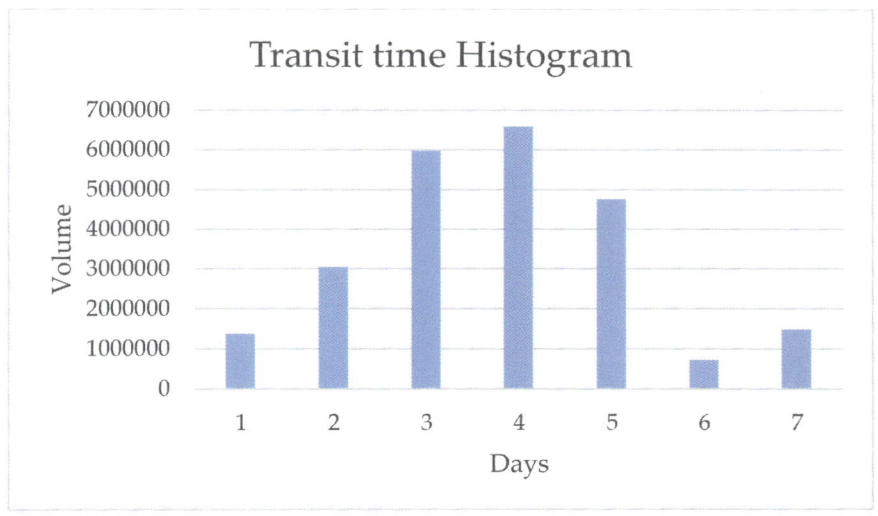

Contour plot (3D/2D)

Sometimes you need to demonstrate the relationship between more than 2 variables. Most charts has only two axis; X and Y. Contour plot has another axis in the third dimension, Z. The X and Y factors are plotted on the X and Y axis respectively, while the response is plotted in the Z axis. Magnitudes of the response are represented by different color bands, similar to a topographical map. Contour plots are easily plotted using Excel or other statistical tools. It can be plotted as a 3D chart for those who are more acquainted with seeing things in 3 dimensions. Here's an example of a 2D plot showing how factory capacity and buffer levels are influencing air shipments. In this case 20% factory capacity upside with a +15% buffer will give 6%-8% of air shipments.

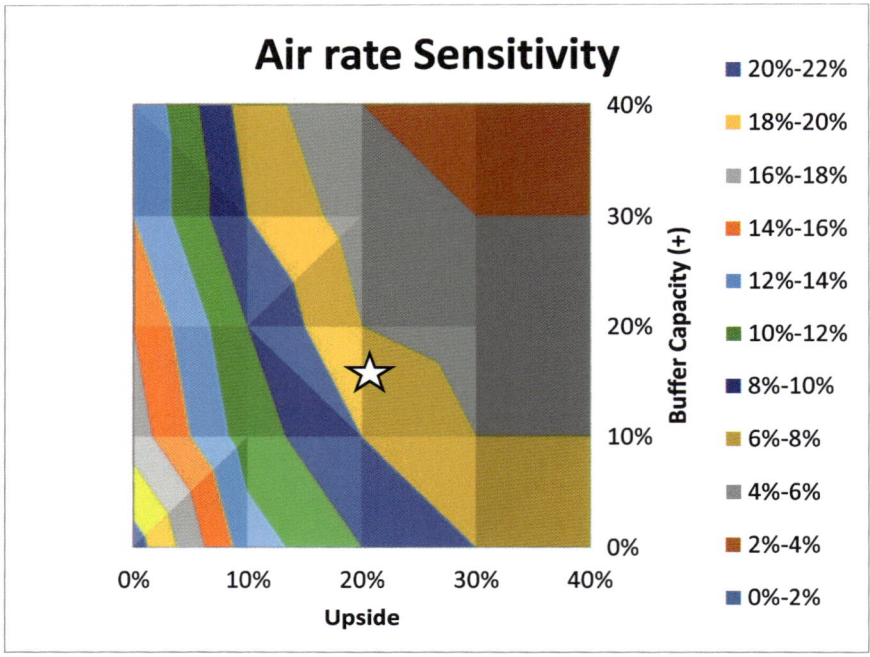

Proportion / Comparison

A very common data study is to identify differences in performance between different choice point e.g. Carriers, ports etc. Column charts are good representation of such information as categorical data can be plotted side by side for relative visual comparison. They are few variants of column chart and are used to show different types of information such as individual category (Clustered), totality (Stacked) or 100% stacked (Ratio).

Here are a few examples demonstrating representation of same information using different types of column charts.

    i.   Using clustered column chart, comparison of the product shipment volume by day of the week over 3 years was done. Thursday shipments formed the major volume

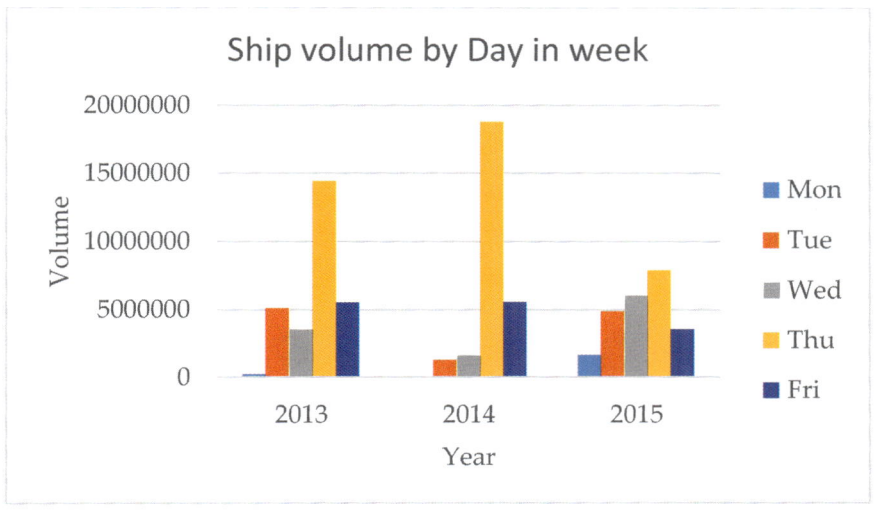

ii. The data can be re-arranged to show the trend changes over time. The trend shows a significant reduction of Thursday shipments from 2013 to 2015. You can either compare the total volume over time, or by changing the first chart to a stacked column (See next graph).

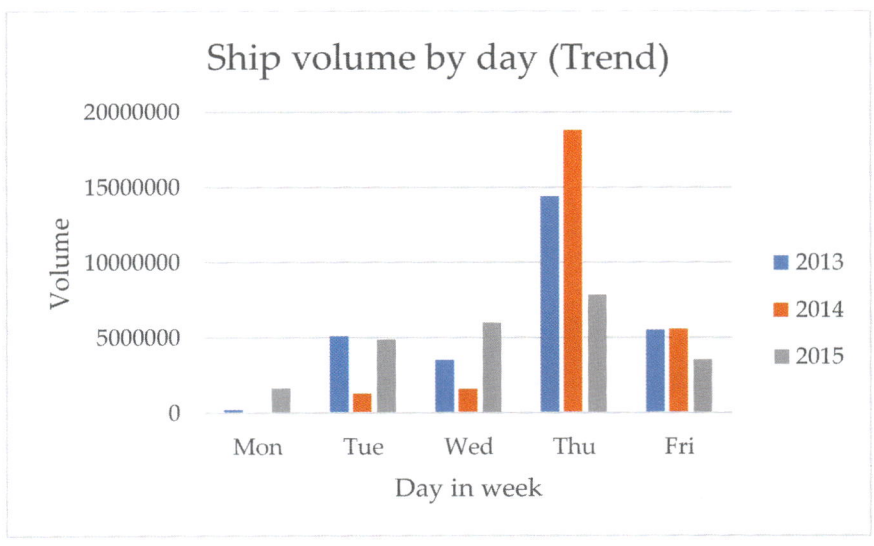

iii. Here the data is stacked to show the combine trend over time. It is now pretty obvious that shipment volume has dropped over time. The previous chart also shows a shift from high Thursday shipments to a more equal spread of shipments from Tuesday to Thursday.

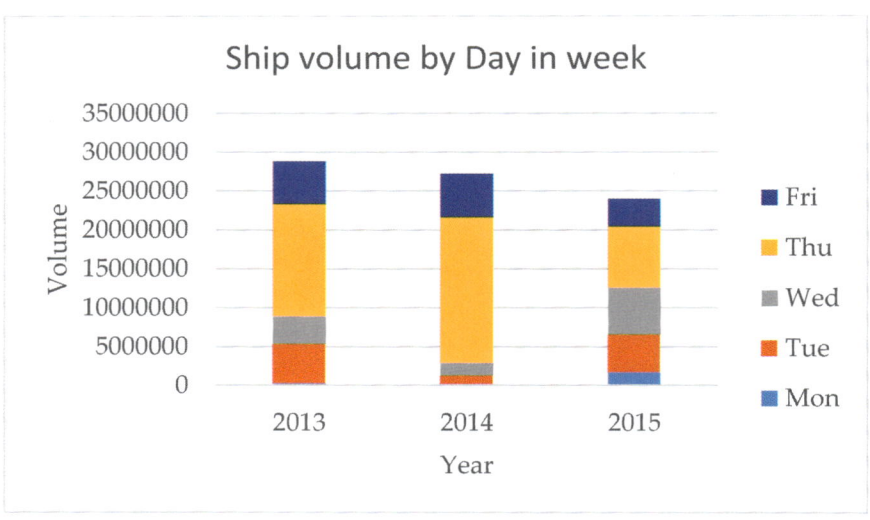

Heat Table / Heat Map

Heat table/Maps are useful in showing area where problem tends to happen. Heat maps are a form of matrix table or geographical map where the events of occurrences are represented by different colors. Through the map you will be able to identify area where the most intensified activities are happening e.g. epidemic on a geographical map, frequency of electrical test failure on a wafer map and etc. Many visual analytic tools offer the option to plot the geographical concentration of events. You can easily find the basic version for free online as well.

Below is a sample of how heat table was used to identify the occurrences of customers' backlog over a period of time by product type, using Excel. This was part of an on-going process to monitor the effectiveness of safety stock settings. Within Excel, you can use conditional formatting feature to highlight high frequency cells as red and the lower one as green. We have used the same feature with the grey tone for the illustration. The darker tone represents area of high occurrences of backlog. What you can see from the table are indications of higher backlog across most products from Week 30 onwards. Upon checking against the calendar it shows that the period represents the quarter end month of August. Further analysis shows forthcoming price changes were driving resellers capitalizing the last minute purchase using the old pricing. This was causing a surge in demand and creating product stock out situation. As this is pretty much event driven, the usual safety stock level would not have been able to protect against the spike. This should be mitigated through a better forecast in future when similar event transpires again.

Part	WK27	WK28	WK29	WK30	WK31	WK32	WK33	WK34
NC140	0	0	0	121	4	0	2	0
CH456	0	0	40	6	39	77	2	0
CB874	0	0	0	0	0	101	62	0
CC600	0	0	0	0	11	21	10	52
CC874	0	0	0	0	0	30	85	1
C8771	27	4	0	0	0	0	0	0
BB321	0	0	0	0	0	82	4	1
C6614	0	0	0	0	49	0	0	0
C9514	0	0	0	0	29	15	0	0
C9314	0	0	0	0	0	0	46	0
D8614	0	0	0	0	0	35	0	0

Below is a second scenario showing the heat map of silicon wafers electrical failures. Data is collected from a single tool which demonstrated higher failures than the rest. The positions of failure were tracked manually on a spreadsheet containing wafer map. Each time a failure occurs on that position the score will be accumulated. After sufficient sample are gathered, we used the accumulated score to review where the common failures are happening. It is evident that the failure tends to be on the upper right corner. This helped the team to identify levelling issue with the wafer equipment as the root cause.

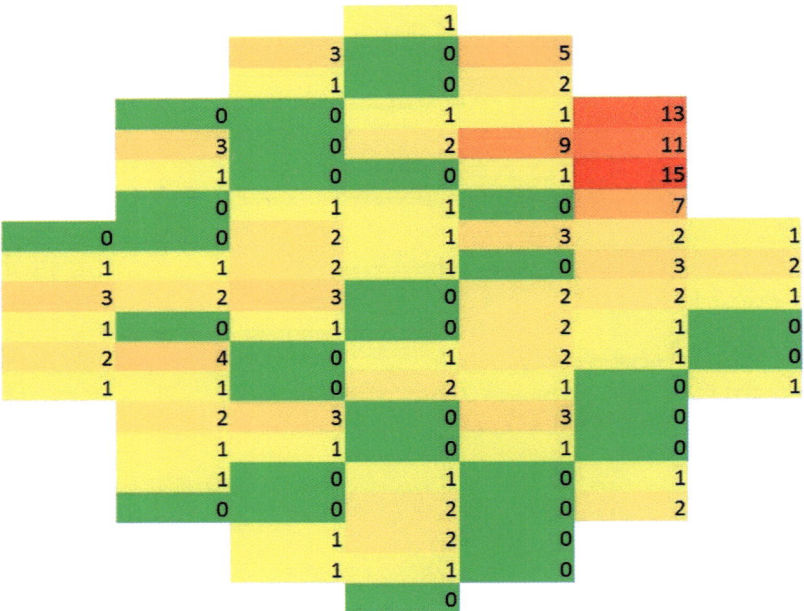

As you can see, you can use several types of charts for different purpose of analysis and building your observations. More sophisticated charting tools are made available today especially with the development of more visualization tools as compared to in the past. The above examples are the most common and fundamental techniques required for building your visual analytical skills. We hope the information presented will help you build a solid foundation for visual analysis.

g. Descriptive statistic / Quantitative analysis

We often need a way to summarize big amount of data using simple yet concise parameters. This is where descriptive statistic is used to summarize and quantify the data on hand. Statistics such as standard deviation, mean, median, skewness, correlation coefficient etc. provides key characteristic information about the data. Extending beyond visual analysis, we further compile descriptive test and analysis on the given data to prove its statistical importance. Not only that, we can also run test to compare performance between the populations of data. See the two charts below as an example:-

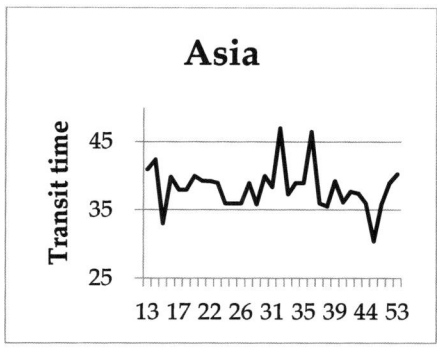 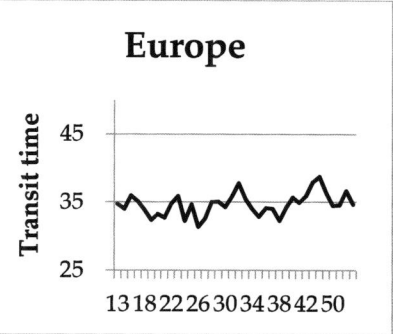

Qualitative observation shows that the parts shipped from Asia have higher standard deviation in Transit time. To prove it statistically we can run an F test using any of the statistical software available. The F-test test if two population variances are equal by comparing the ratio of two variances. So, if the variances are equal, the ratio of the variances will be 1. All hypothesis testing is done under the assumption the null hypothesis is true. Performing an F-test in Excel rejects the Null hypothesis, confirming the difference in variance is significant (F>F Critical one tail).

F-Test Two-Sample for Variances

	Asia	Europe
Mean	38.28046485	34.32029925
Variance	10.24393356	3.071882467
Observations	33	43
df	32	42
F	3.334741375	
P(F<=f) one-tail	0.000152347	
F Critical one-tail	1.718078659	

A similar ANOVA (Analysis of Variance) test can be conducted to test the Mean for the two sets of data by analyzing variance. In this case since the variances are quite different we used the t-test assuming unequal variance. The test result rejects the Null hypothesis that both Mean are comparable (t Stat not within +/- t Critical two-tail).

t-Test: Two-Sample Assuming Unequal Variances

	Asia	*Europe*
Mean	38.21682084	33.79868531
Variance	10.43640266	2.326909478
Observations	32	32
Hypothesized Mean Difference	0	
df	44	
t Stat	6.995718528	
P(T<=t) one-tail	5.79899E-09	
t Critical one-tail	1.680229977	
P(T<=t) two-tail	1.1598E-08	
t Critical two-tail	2.015367574	

The key concept of descriptive statistic is that it helps you to determine the statistical properties of the data. It not only quantifies but also differentiates between the different populations of data samples. Through the result, we are able to make further inference and comparison confidently, avoiding any guessing.

h. Result validation

After building and testing your hypothesis, the next critical step is to validate your findings with a subject matter expert (SME). The SME should have been identified at the start of the analysis and is someone who is knowledgeable in the subject of study and is able to provide more contexts on the key findings. Other sources of validation could include the internet, process documentation, historical dashboard and even system domain expertise.

Validation is important for a few reasons:-

    i.   We need to know what the underlying root causes to the problem are. Interviewing the SME will help to validate your findings, and also lead you into the root cause. Ask the 5 W's and H to the SME (Why, Who, When, What, Where and How). After a few layers of onion peeling, you will reach the answer you were seeking.

    ii.   Stakeholders need to gain the confidence on your model and assumptions. They will check your assumptions or result through triangulating with facts they already know e.g. volume, historical

iii. SME are another source of validation for the stakeholders. It is very important to align with the SME on the findings before broader sharing. The last thing you want to happen is the SME disagreeing with you during that important stakeholders sharing.
iv. There are times when the data findings are counter-intuitive and may also disagree with the documented processes. Actual practices are often quite different from the documented guidelines. Be ready with data and validate with SME before sharing your results.

In a nutshell, keep asking yourself questions that you might be asked. Be well prepared to share your validation data as it will certainly help lay the path for a more productive discussion.

i. Present findings and proposals

Rounding up all your findings and presenting it to the stakeholders is the most crucial stage of the process. The most challenging part is how you connect all the dots and present the story in an easy to understand and yet concise way. Presentation to different audience will require different contents and levels of details. Your manager will have a heavy interest in the engineering details, especially the validation of your analysis. It is their role to ensure result accuracy and validation prior to it getting communicated to the next level of management tier. However when it comes to sharing with higher management stakeholder, you need to trim down the content for methodology and validation. The content should be kept minimum to just results and key takeaways which is referred as executive summary. Here's the recommended format:-

1) Objective and scope
2) Data scope and Methodology (Trim for different audiences)
3) Validation result (Trim for different audiences)
4) Insights, findings
5) Recommendations and Path Forward

Objective and Scope

A project objective should be only a few concise statements spelling out the intended outcome of the project. Objective should be specific, must be tangible, and includes the agreed timeline. The scope of study should also be agreed and spelled out so that there are no questions about it at a later stage.

Data scope and Methodology

Data scoping is a frequently asked question. There might be a question around why certain data span was included or excluded. You would have done sufficient data analysis by this stage that enables you to provide enough justification on why certain data are included or excluded. Older data might be excluded for the reason that rapid business condition changes made the data not representative of the current situation anymore. The pre-defined project scope will also help to set the framework for choosing what data is to be used.

You will also want to put up a 1 page summary of sample analyses. This should be a concise summary in comparison to what you share with your immediate manager. The key idea is to share with stakeholders a quick takeaways message that includes the tools, ideas, hypotheses that forms the backbone of the result you are going to share. Always keep to layman terms and includes key takeaway messages for the information you are sharing. Graphical trends and visual dashboards are always better than tables and long list of numbers.

Validation data

You have built a model, made some observations and are trying to prove a hypothesis. As a proof point to the accuracy of analysis, you need to be able to share with stakeholders evidences of the tests and validations done prior to sharing. Most times discovered problems seems counter-intuitive at first. It should be, else it will not be a problem that requires your analysis. Stakeholders will have the same challenge and has to be convinced by you. You should always use empirical data, events or new data that is gathered to prove your result. A comparison of predictive vs actuals will be a good gauge, and information should be represented in simple graphical form as much as possible. Remember, a confused audience will mean more doubts than agreement with your hard work.

Insights

Here's where your analysis adds a lot of value. A good analyst does not just report the problem, but finds the root cause and recommend solutions. This is where you can expect to spend most of your time for your presentations to the stakeholders. This is when you breakdown your analyses and quantify the various problems and impacts. Insights should be filtered and only those that are potentially beneficial to the organization should be presented. You would have more underlying root causes and findings that others don't see. Be sure to keep the list to the important and impactful ones.

Recommendation and Path Forward

If you are sick, you want a drug prescription to help you to recover. It doesn't help the business to merely understand where it is failing, but they are counting on you to identify from your data suggestions for improvement. This section is where you present your proposed solution. Your solution may include projections of cost and choice points for stakeholder to make the decision. You may also need to set a time for the team to meet again after collecting the post implementation data, and officially close the study.

Implementation and Control

The process of implementation does not fall within the scope of data analyses, but successful implementation and follow through should be the last step to complete the project. We recommend setting a reporting mechanism to monitor the success metric after project implementation. Six Sigma DMAIC framework emphasize greatly on having a control mechanism in place after implementation. A control mechanism can be a metric designed to monitor the quality of the improvements, such as reports. Metric not only serve as a triggering mechanism for actions against performance deterioration, but also serves as a mechanism to induce diligence in people running the process.

CHAPTER 5

ANALYSIS 101

"Best practices and case studies…"

When we were designing the content for this book, we decided to not only teach the technique but also help you avoid some potential issues by leveraging our real world analytical experience. In this section we are going to share with you some common mistakes people make, which can completely change the outcome of the analysis. Here are the few topics we will be discussing:-

    i. Using absolute vs Relative
    ii. Arithmetic vs Ratio
    iii. Mean vs Median
    iv. Limitation of simulation software

Absolute vs Relative

We were recently asked to build a predictive tool for a Logistic team. The transit time for the product shipment was deteriorating, and so there was a dire need to understand the factors behind the issue. We were asked to build a model to predict future transit time based on the outcome of root cause findings.

The data file contained historical transit time goal vs actuals transit time. A positive delta meant actual was higher than goal (failures), while negative values meant transit time was meeting the goal. The team proposed to build a Logistic model that could predict pass/fail based on the given data. Let's pause for a moment and think on the request.

Let's recap the purpose and objective of the tool again. The task was to build a predictive model that could help to predict the next transit delay so that timely mitigation actions could be put in place. Mitigation actions can be step such as shipping the products earlier, or adding buffer to cater for the effects caused by the delays. Having a model that simply tells you pass/fail doesn't help you quantify the delay nor provide insights to how much additional buffer is needed. Another problem was with the target transit time being a dynamic number that changed based on actual performance over time. The target was changed twice in the past 3 years. So the same shipment would have different delta at different point of time when different targets were used. The baseline shouldn't be using a moving target. Based on this new knowledge, the team accepted that it was necessary to build a model that predict the actual transit time than a Logistic model that uses a moving baseline as passing criteria.

Arithmetic vs Ratio

Here's a chart showing the number of failures over time. The Y-axis represents the failure count over a period of time.

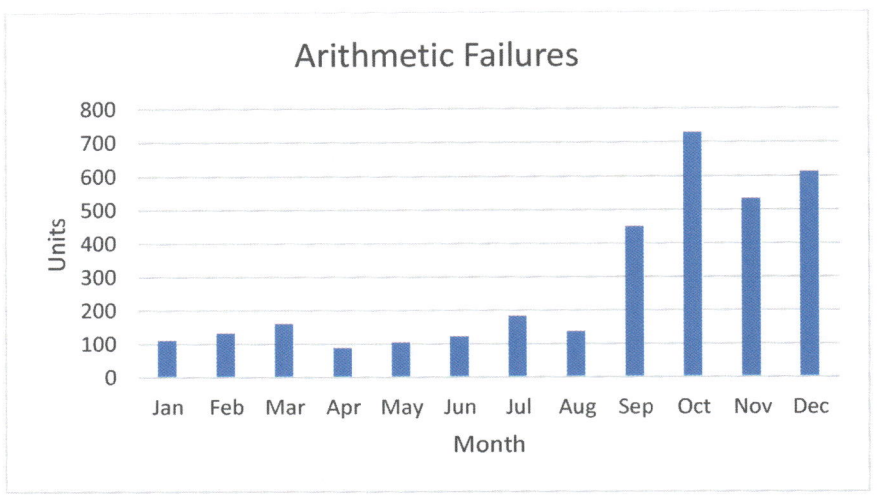

The initial observation shows that the failure counts started to increase rapidly from the period of September onwards. One may strongly recommend a round of investigation to determine what went wrong during that period. In most cases, we usually plot absolute count of a particular event without considering that the volume of events might varies from time to time. Including another perspective that shows the absolute count data as a ratio of the total event count will normalize the data to give a better comparison between the data groupings.

Here's how the chart looks like once we take the ratio of failures against the total volume during each period.

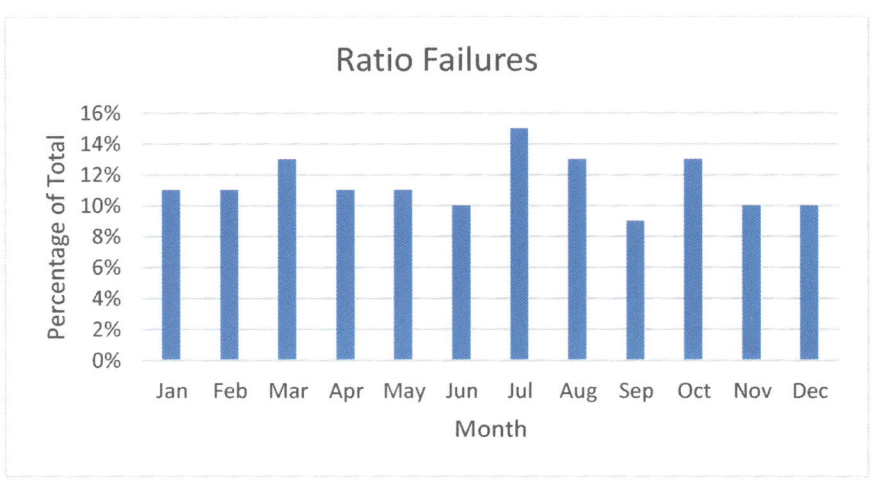

Well, now the story looks completely different. The initial data was showing higher failures starting September onwards, but that was due to the higher shipment volume. The percentage of error actually did not deteriorate.

Mean vs Median

We commonly calculate and represent the Mean value for a given set of data. Mean calculation has a known flaw. A high or low outlier number in your dataset could very well skew the mean of the data. This will especially be prominent if your data set is small, or the outlier data is having a big difference in values compared to the rest of the data. To overcome this challenge we recommend performing the Median calculation. Median shows the value of the middle data points, so essentially even if you have a big outlier in either or both ends of your data, Median values will not change. We recommend using Mean calculation together with Median. Whenever there is a huge difference in Mean vs Median, it indicates that the data has outlier. You can use this method to detect problem in the data as well.

Using modeling software

Supply chain complexity is growing as more contract manufacturing and distribution network expand in sizes. Data collection and analysis has become an important core activity for companies to keep up with the growing customer segments demanding enhanced speed. Simulation software fit into the space of providing easy to use platform turning around supply chain analysis at a significantly shorter time.

As with any analysis, the accuracy of the modeling or simulation is only as accurate as the given input. Tools are designed to meet different levels of needs and support various types of study. There are however some limitations in the tools which we are going to highlight through examples here. You may be using different tools, however high likelihood they suffer from the similar limitations as most tools are fundamentally designed similarly. Hopefully, with this knowledge you start considering tool limitations when building your next data modeling task. Here's what we have observed in some of the tools we used:-

> i. Supply chain network modeling tools uses forecast accuracy at the last customer node. Forecast accuracy is aggregated and populated upstream to all the nodes, using statistical pooling formula. What is happening in the real world is that each node in supply chain is adding varied complexity and influencing behavior of the overall system. Human intervention and behavior adds further complexity. Variation grows in magnitude (Bullwhip effect) further upstream of the supply chain and so some of

ii. these problems might actually be underestimated by the tool, and so have an impact on the outcome. If you are well versed with your own supply chain network, you may be either able to build your own simulation to overcome or validate this issue.

ii. Similar to the example above, the other issue is about factoring correlation into the model. To illustrate this, let's use an example. Component A is used in the production of two engines, X and Y. It was observed that when demand for X increases, demand for Y decreases. This is a classic case of negative correlation. The good news is that modeling tools do provides an option to input collinearity, however the problem is that it takes some effort to define the magnitude of the collinearity when patterns are appearing randomly. In real world practice, we often introduce quarter end promotions that completely distort the natural order pattern by the customers. Therefore if you look at the data you will start to see different behaviors across various time periods. The most accurate and easy way to calculate the variance is to actually combines the demand for both X and Y for the same period, and then calculate the variation using the aggregated demand data.

Off the shelf tools have several merits and are valuable assets, however it's important to understand their limitations and assumptions prior to using them to your advantage.

Supply Chain case studies

ERP process

Organizations spend lot of effort in setting the right safety stock to protect against stressful stocking out situation. However, how effective usually the safety stock setup strategy is?

Jane works as a planner for an electronic manufacturing company and is in charge of setting the correct safety stock at the distribution center in North America. Jane performs weekly planning, uses ERP software that flags out any forthcoming potential stock-out situation, and propose shipment plans accordingly to ensure product availability in the region. The default shipment goes via ocean, and when the demand spikes, air shipments were triggered to accelerate replenishment to prevent a stock-out situation.

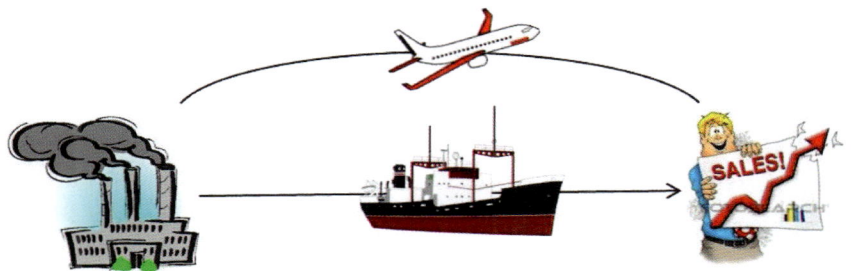

Her planning director is concerned with the high number of air shipments and is reviewing what it takes to cut down the amount of air shipments thereby avoiding additional amount incurred on shipments. Knowing that sufficient safety stock should have already been catered for the regions, the director is unable to figure out why the company is still incurring air shipments now and then. Is it because safety stock setting is not thorough or accurate enough?

Let's start by first understanding how the replenishment system actually works. ERP software nets incoming shipments and on hand inventory against forecast and customer orders. When the net result is negative, ERP system looks for alternatives to prevent the stock-out situation and that includes air shipment. Does the ERP system consider targeted service level during the netting process? No, the system sole purpose is to ensure there is no stock-out with the goal of 100% availability.

You probably would have noticed the gap by now. You don't set safety stock for 100% availability and theoretically 100% service level is not even possible. The efficient frontier for setting safety stock service level falls in the range of 95% to 98%. Beyond this it will take significant investment in safety stock to gain you another percent gain in the service level. The customer was expecting the company in providing 95% service level for their orders, which was indeed considered by the company while setting safety stock in the region. This means the operation is ready to miss 5% of the orders, but that's not how the ERP software makes replenishment decisions. The system has been designed to prevent backlog and is expecting 100% service level, and hence will propose air shipments whenever needed. Since we only setup safety stock for 95% service level, we will continue to see system proposing air shipments. The result is a higher service level at the expense of air shipment. This impact will be greater when the service level chosen for the safety stock is lower. There is no automated solution to this problem and one way is to simply trust the safety stock to service 95% of the orders and put a halt to all air shipments. The director decided to slowly reduce the unit of air shipments as this was a less risky change management decision. The result; air shipments were reduced by half without impacting availability goal.

Modeling of air shipments

Companies spend significant amount of money annually on air freights. In this section we will discuss one of the simulation model we built using Excel that simulates air shipments for different replenishment strategies. As you read more, you will realize that most of the examples we are covering not just offer solutions for real world supply chain issues, but we also shares problems that you cannot easily simulate using standard supply chain software. This is reason we want you to be aware of the limitation of off-the shelf tools. Also, this ability is what differentiates a simulation tool user from a supply chain business expert that we hope you become. In this example, the final solution helped the supply chain director to identify opportunities and quantify the impact of various choice points to service level and air shipments.

The default shipment mode to the distribution center is via Ocean. Customers usually place orders 1 to 2 weeks in advance before the required delivery date. Beyond that time horizon the factories relies on forecast to build and ship via ocean mode. Customer expects service level to be 95% and accordingly with that goal in mind, safety stock is designed. When demand fluctuates and stock-out of inventories in distribution center is projected, air shipments are activated.

Different practices are followed when it comes to air replenishment quantities. Some factory planners replenish just enough to prevent a stock-out, while others prefer to replenish stock back to safety stock level.

The supply chain director is keen to understand the differences in air replenishment method (replenishing to prevent stock-out versus replenishing to safety stock level), and how it impact the service level, if any. The task require us to determine what the correct practice is, and then use that as a standardized guide for all the planners and hopefully thereby reducing spending on air shipments.

Here's a pictorial representation of the model built in Excel. We derived historical forecast error from past data and used that to simulate our own random demand coming from customer. User of the simulation tool can choose between replenishment just enough to prevent stock-out or fill up to the safety stock level. The output is a measurement of air shipments and corresponding service level, affected by the choice point of the respective replenishment methods. Model assumed that factory had sufficient upside to support the amount of increased demand.

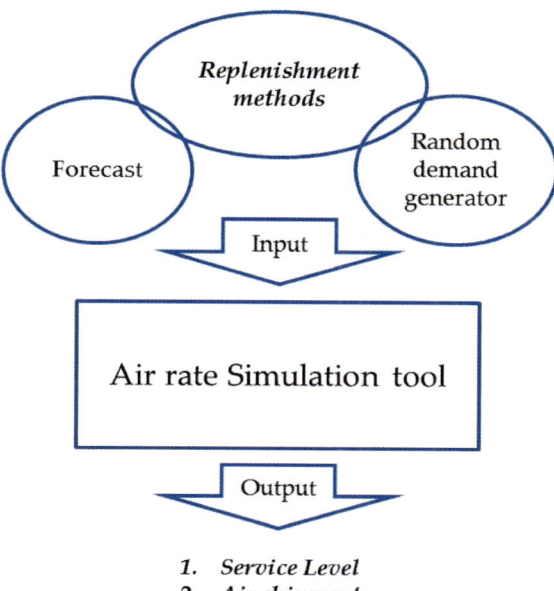

Here's the final output after running the simulation model for several iterations.

Replenishment Method	Air to prevent backlog	Air to Safety stock
Air rate	1%	6%
Service Level	95.70%	97.20%

The following conclusions can be made here.

i. Air shipment to prevent backlog scenario is sufficient to maintain 95% goal
ii. Shipping to safety stock level increased air shipments significantly, as compared to the marginal increase in service level. The additional air shipments was not necessary to meet service level goal.

It may seem counter-intuitive to see a small increment in service level despite a 5% increase in air shipments. Firstly, factory takes 1 week to react and another week for air freight to reach the region. Immediate demand spike can happen even before the air shipments arrive, and so in fact some of the air shipments are not really helping to prevent the backlog in the first place. Also mentioned earlier, replenishment decisions were also based on forecast. Over-forecasting could also lead to false alarm triggering air shipment decisions. The director was happy with the result and this new replenishment strategy help saved the company tremendous amount of money on unnecessary air shipments each year.

Factory capacity sizing
In the previous example we saw how air shipment decision affects the operating cost of a company. The answer couldn't have been possible without using analytic and a clear understanding of the process.

In this example we shall be discussing a very key fundamental question people always struggle to find the right answer: - How much additional capacity upside should I keep? Adding capacity comes at a cost as it involves investing in additional capital equipment and staffing. So, how do we quantify how much is needed before making the financial decision?

Upside requirements depends on several factors. For those supply chain that uses both air and ocean shipments, upside requirements are usually cushioned by using air as temporary measure for recovery against unforeseen demand spikes. This allows lower upside but with a tradeoff of higher air shipments. For a supply chain that has only one mode of shipment, the supply chain is directly coupled to the downstream demand. For such a supply chain, you will be required to maintain an upside to respond and match the magnitude of demand swing.

As mentioned above, having two or more modes of shipment allows more flexibility in setting the upside requirement. However, it does come at a cost. When we use air shipments for recovery against high demand, it cost the business more money in expediting. This is a classic case study between balancing of capital investment versus operational cost.

Before we build the simulation model, let's start by understanding some fundamentals which are the building blocks needed for simulation.

    i.   Capacity upside is a function of the magnitude of demand variation i.e. higher forecast error requires higher upside from the supply nodes

ii. Capacity upside depends on whether there is more than 1 mode of shipping, we need to understand and quantify the trade-off between expedite versus maintaining higher upside capital
iii. For single mode of shipment, upside requirement is equal to the amount of demand swing. Safety stock does helps cushion the effect of demand spike, but not sustainable if factory does not have capacity to replenish it back to healthy level. So let's assume safety stock is supposed to be kept constant.
iv. For multiple mode of shipment
    a. If upside is available for the demand spike, factory builds the additional quantity and ship the parts using air mode
    b. If demand spike is higher than available upside, factory has to converts some of the scheduled current ocean shipments into air mode. This leaves void in the subsequent ocean replenishment, and this is a void that will be filled later using more air shipments. This also means higher air shipments compared to if higher capacity upside was available.
    c. Air shipments is inversely proportionally to capacity upside, and saturates off when upside is equivalent to demand spike (Expected outcome of the model)
v. Stock-out will continue to happen if demand spike goes on for prolong period. The time to recovery will depends on the magnitude of demand spike versus the amount of factory upside over a period of time
vi. Summarize from above
    Air shipments = f(Demand variability, demand bias, factory upside)

Finally, here's the result of one the model we built.

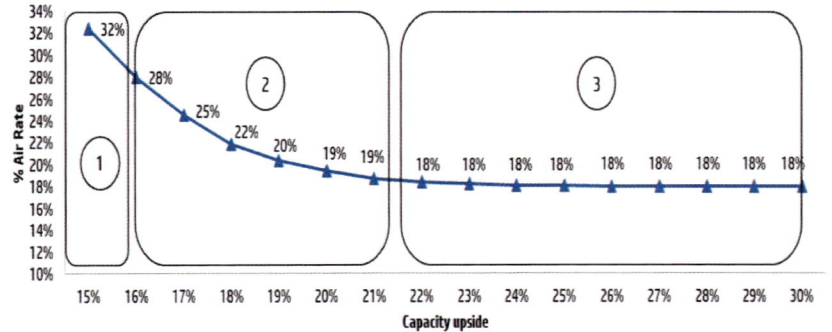

There are 3 zones identified in the graph.

Zone 1 – This is when capacity upside is insufficient to match the demand spike. Air shipments and stock-out is high. You do not wish to size your factory capacity this way.

Zone 2 – This is the capacity zone wherein you would make decision considering trade-off between capital investments versus cost of air shipments. As capacity upside improves, air shipments decreases and stabilizes towards a saturation point.

Zone 3 – This is where capacity upside matches the upside in demand. Pushing capacity upside higher does not gain you any improvements in air shipments. To reduce the air shipments beyond this point requires consideration of other strategies such as increasing buffer stock, improving forecast accuracy and etc.

We know that each supply chain is different, and forecast accuracy between products at maturity versus growth stage is not going to be the same. As there was not really a standard statistical method to determine the optimized upside, the golden rule used by this particular manufacturing supply chain was to maintain a 15% capacity upside across all the production processes. In this particular example we noted higher than usual demand variation. The model suggested maintaining an upside of ~21% could results in the lowest air shipments. It turned out that there was no additional capital investment required, by just adding staffing we could increase current upside to 21%. Further financial study confirmed that it was more cost effective to increase the current staffing level and keep the air shipments lower. The model became a new standard for analyzing factory capacity upside requirement, and we were asked to perform similar study across other product portfolio.

Factory capacity sizing, air shipments and Buffer

Buffering is a costly but convenient solution against supply chain inefficiencies. Inventory buffers affects cash flow and often leads to potential scrap, devaluation and other issues. Keeping low buffer on the other hand, requires a highly responsive supply chain that performs frequent review of inventory positions and execute quick stock out recovery which may involves using air shipments. Also, factories are more susceptible to demand fluctuation when buffer are lean, as buffer recovery are only possible if there are ample supplies. These elements are intertwined and require an optimization model to strike a good balance, which brings us to the next customized simulation model.

So far, we have explained and showcase examples looking at how each single supply chain factor impacts air shipments and vice versa. You may be wondering if we can expand this model further and incorporate more factors. Answer is yes. As usual we will start by first explaining the end to end supply chain flow, and how supply chain response to the volatility in demand.

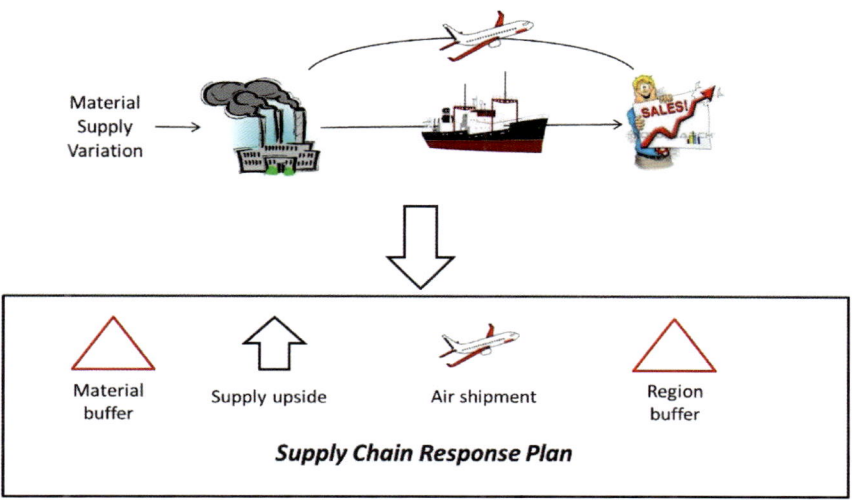

Let's review how each of the response plan helps to maintain availability to customers.

Region buffer – This buffer is setup to maintain healthy product availability to end customers. Factories are usually far and replenishments take time to reach the region. In such situation factory always produces to forecast, and we need a local buffer in the regional distribution center to cushion the demand spike. We have a separate topic discussing how to setup the right buffer size, so for now let's assume the stock has been setup appropriately.

Air shipments – Parts have to be air shipped to the regions when demand comes in much stronger than anticipated, or when there is a last minute promotional event that was not forecasted. A supply chain with long replenishment lead-time tends to be subjected to this impact since replenishment takes time. Businesses typically run promotion at end of quarter or financial year so that they could catch up with the last minute financial gap. Such abrupt decisions are made quite late and demand information is only made available towards the very end to the factories. By that time decision is made, it will be too late for factory to react and ship the parts and so it has to be expedited. This is why air shipments are usually high towards quarter end.

Factory supply upside – Buffer are just like water wells. As consumption spikes, you need to turn on the tap (Factory production) to fill the water back up to the level. As we mentioned earlier supply upside not only affects the air shipments, but also the ability to replenish the demand so you are not caught with a stock-out situation.

Material buffer – Material buffer works the similar way as buffer in the region. Material buffer can be managed efficiently through supplier partnership. With proper setup and contractual agreement, materials buffer can be carried by supplier. There are several options available to dictate the arrangement but due to the scope of the topic we will not discuss it here.

We were asked to build a model to simulate the complex relationship between factories capacity upside, air shipments and buffer level in the region. This will be an important study since traditionally each supply chain organization builds their own optimization. We needed a view that could help balance end to end, striking a balance between availability, cost and inventory.

The model was again built in Excel, since we didn't find an existing simulation package available for such study. As usual let's start with describing some building blocks of the model.
  i. Inputs to the model:-
      a. Historical forecast error, quantify by coefficient of variant (COV). More on COV will be discussed latter in detail in the calculation of Safety stock topic.
      b. Review frequency
      c. Replenishment lead-time
      d. Factory capacity upside
      e. Region buffer level

  ii. We will be building a sequential replenishment routine
      a. Each routine will have forward looking forecast based on latest plan, and a simulated actual demand based on historical COV (Forecast error)
      b. Replenishment quantity for each routine will be to get the inventory back to the targeted Regional buffer level
      c. Potential backlog within ocean replenishment lead-time will be replenished using Air shipments instead
      d. Demand will be replenished in full whenever factory capacity allows, or else demand will be carried to the next period of planning if factory capacity is limited

iii. Outputs of the model:-
   a. Air shipments
   b. Availability / service level

iv. Simulation scenarios
   a. Simulate a combination of input values for Factory capacity upside and Regional buffer level
   b. For each combination, run the model multiple times, record the average Service level and Air shipments

Two separate tables were generated, one to record service level for each combination of Factory capacity upside versus Regional buffer, and another one for the Air shipments. Here's a sample of both the results.

Air shipments

Air		Factory Upside				
		0%	10%	20%	30%	40%
Buffer Capacity	0%	21%	13%	10%	8%	7%
	+10%	17%	11%	8%	6%	6%
	+20%	16%	10%	6%	5%	5%
	+30%	14%	8%	5%	4%	4%
	+40%	14%	7%	4%	3%	3%

The above result shows how air shipments differs for a different combination of factory upside against buffer capacity. Buffers by default are designed for 95% service level, in this case we are testing air shipments by increasing the buffer as an option. You can see that air shipments is saturating towards 3%-4% and any further increase in factory upside or buffer did not bring further reductions in the air shipments. Let's see the same information in a graphical view.

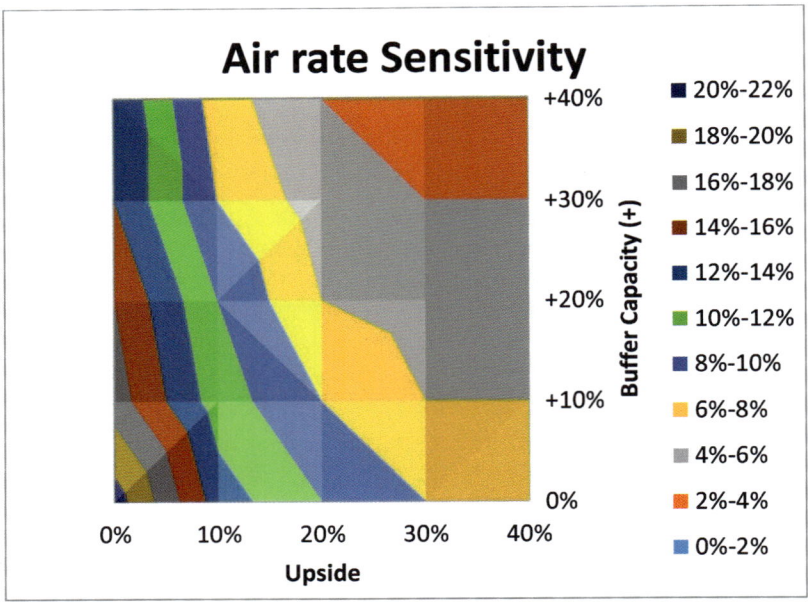

Above is the contour plot representing the same information shown in the previous Air shipments table. On contour plots, the distance between grids represents the gradient/sensitivity. You can easily notice the rate of change towards the top right is more gentle than to the bottom left. Therefore you will expects a bigger return in air shipments reduction at the beginning (bottom left of graph), but as more resources are invested, the returns gets saturated (minimizing returns). As a stakeholder, you can also pick your desired air shipments and determine how you wish to tradeoff between buffer and the factory capacity upside. For example, a 6%-8% air shipments can be achieved if factory upside is 30% and buffer at current level, or at 10% factory upside, but increasing the region buffer by another 30%.

Service level

Service Level		Factory Upside				
		0%	10%	20%	30%	40%
Buffer Capacity	0%	96%	99%	99%	99%	99%
	+10%	98%	99%	99%	99%	99%
	+20%	98%	99%	99%	99%	99%
	+30%	98%	99%	99%	99%	100%
	+40%	98%	99%	99%	99%	100%

Above table shows the service level impact with different combination of factory upsides and buffer levels. What you can quickly notice is that service level increases when factory increases its upside, or similar gain can be achieved by increasing buffer in the region. A similar contour plot is shown below.

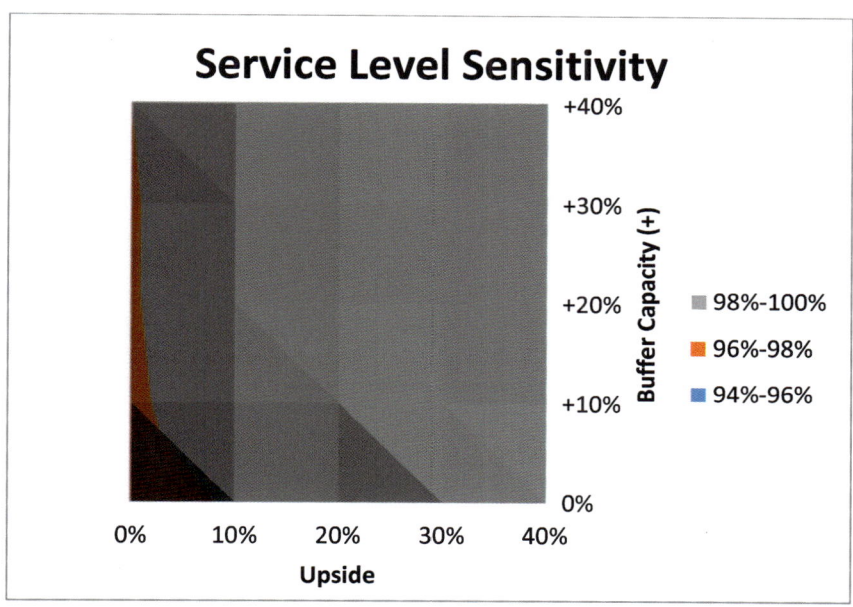

For this case study air shipments was the central improvement driver. It was evident that service level was meeting the 95% requirement, so any further need for improvement would have to be driven by real needs. The choice point between increasing factory upside versus buffer needs further financial analysis. In certain cases, increasing 10% factory capacity might means adding a new production line and costing millions of dollars. In such case adding buffer perhaps is a more economical choice. There are also other ways to improve the situation, such as:-

    i.   Using this information to explore and drive productivity improvement opportunities in the factory and achieve required upside at a fraction of the cost
    ii.   Improves current baseline by better enhancing forecast accuracy

Quantitative studies like above helps to set the stage for meaningful discussions. In many situations it is difficult for each supply chain department to align if they continued to be measured using localize metric. Putting a story that paints the end to end view help the higher level management aligns the whole team in achieving a common goal. Being able to quantify the benefits is the key element that helps when it comes to prioritization and getting focus from stakeholders.

Range of coverage settings in MRP
MRP uses two methods to procure and protects against forecast errors:-

  i. Coverage Profile (Statistical coverage)
  ii. Safety stock (Static quantity)

Depending on the demand volatility you may choose a different mode of safety stock. In general comparison, coverage profile is a dynamic stocking method which changes the quantity based on the forecast. This is typically used in environment where demand is dynamic (Increasing or decreasing), and you have a relatively good forecast that trends with the demand. Safety stock on the other hand is more static. Until you refresh the number, it does not cater for the changes in volume over time. In a dynamic environment you either choose to use coverage profile or refresh the safety stock on a regular basis.

It may appear that being dynamic coverage profile offers advantage over setting a static target; however in practice we witnessed few potential risks using this method for replenishment. Let's go deeper into the topic and we shall use an actual case to illustrate the potential risk and limitation using coverage profile.

Coverage Profile Calculation
Coverage profile calculates the daily average forward looking demand by considering the current and the next 12 weeks of forecast (Based on system settings). The total demand for 13 weeks is aggregated into daily demand, and coverage profile is calculated as ratio of inventory on hand over average daily demand. Coverage profile for each forward looking weeks is calculated the same way, using the projected on hand after deducting for that week's forecast, versus the next 13 weeks average daily forecast. MRP will review the calculated coverage profile within purchase lead-time, and recommends an order if the value is lower than the desired target.

Here's an example.

Lead-time (4 weeks)	Wk1	Wk2	Wk3	Wk4	Wk5	Wk6
Forecast	100	100	100	100	100	100
Inventory (End of week)	700	600	500	400	800	700
Coverage profile target (Days)	28	28	28	28	28	28
Projected Coverage (DOS)	49	42	35	28	56	49
Order	500					
Receipt					500	

The lead-time to purchase is 4 weeks in this example. Here we created a simple example where forecast for demand is pretty flat, and coverage profile target is set to 28 days to protect against forecast error. In week 1, MRP look forward and sees that the projected coverage on week 5 is lesser than target, therefore it proposed an order of lot size 500 which is to be delivered by week 5 (According to lead-time of 4 weeks). If you compare the inventory on any week against forecast you can see we managed to maintain at least 28 days of buffer. This works well for a forecast which is relatively flat.

Scenario 1: Below we illustrate a case where forecast was irregular. We saw spike in week 5 and 6, which could be due to promotion event. The spike in forecast did not create a huge requirement for additional buffer since MRP averages the forecast for 13 weeks.

Lead-time (4 weeks)	Wk1	Wk2	Wk3	Wk4	Wk5	Wk6
Forecast	100	100	100	100	500	500
Inventory (End of week)	1000	900	800	700	700	700
Coverage profile target (Days)	28	28	28	28	28	28
Projected Coverage (DOS)	43	39	35	30	30	37
Order	500	500				
Receipt					500	500

As expected MRP saw projected coverage below target and proposed an order of 500 units in week 1 and week 2. Comparing to the last example, here you notice that at the end of week 4, projected coverage is 30 DOS. If you look at the number of units, the inventory of 700 units is only 9 Days of Supply (DOS) against week 5 demand. The method of averaging 13 weeks of forecast doesn't cater well for this situation as we are made to believe that the stock is providing 30 DOS at the end of week 4. The buffer was actually slightly more than a week in this case and this creates a period where we are vulnerable to any further demand spike.

Scenario 2: Below we show another example and this time for a low volume runner product. Forecast quantities for such product are usually 0 for most periods, and production runs on a periodic basis e.g. once a quarter.

Lead-time (4 weeks)	Wk1	Wk2	Wk3	Wk4	Wk5	Wk6
Forecast	0	0	0	0	100	0
Inventory (End of week)	35	35	35	35	85	85
Coverage profile target (Days)	28	28	28	28	28	28
Projected Coverage (DOS)	32	32	32	32	77	77
Order	150					
Receipt					150	

In this example, there is only one production event that is forecasted in week 5. The coverage profile is set to 28 days and so in our minds we are assured that we have one month worth of protection.

Low volume runners have a typical problem of demand uncertainty, and so the timing of build changes all the time. In the following week plan, we realized that the 100 units demand has shifted forward to week 4.

Lead-time (4 weeks)	Wk1	Wk2	Wk3	Wk4	Wk5	Wk6
Forecast	0	0	0	100	0	0
Inventory (End of week)	35	35	35	-65	85	85
Coverage profile target (Days)	28	28	28	28	28	28
Projected Coverage (DOS)	32	32	32	-59	77	77
Order	150					
Receipt					150	

We only have 35 units on hand and out of a sudden are in a potential stock-out situation. Management question why a 28 days coverage profile wasn't sufficient when plan shifted by just 7 days. By now you should be able to answer that.

As illustrated in the above 2 scenarios, coverage profile does not provide good protection in cases where forecast is fairly uneven. In such cases additional safety stock over coverage profile will be required.

EOQ (Economic Order Quantity)

There is always a tradeoff between cost of holding inventory, cost per order and price discount. For components used in lower volume products, we tend to run into the situation of shelf life expiry if orders are in bigger lot sizes. However it's a prevalent practice of achieving savings from bulk buying without considering ramification of scraping off the expired material subsequently. We need a mathematical tool to help provide a system tradeoff of the various cost buckets including potential obsolescence or expiry. Let's start from the well-known century old Wilson formula.

Wilson formula was developed by Ford W. Harris in 1913 but named after the consultant R. H. Wilson who extensively applied the formula. The formula helps to determine the Economic Ordering Quantity (EOQ or Q in the formula). Various inputs are used to determine the EOQ:-

D – Yearly demand in units
S – Cost per order (Admin, transportation etc.)
H – Annual inventory holding cost

$$Q = \sqrt{\frac{2DS}{H}}$$

The formula comes with few assumptions and restrictions.

- Demand are constant through the year
- Fixed ordering cost
- Cost per unit is constant (No price discount for bulk purchase)
- Replenishment for inventory happens when it just touches zero

This is a very basic but fundamental formulation that every buyer needs to be aware and know how to use. In actual practice we might face with a different scenario which requires a little tweak of the formula. For example, the formula does not cater for pricing discount while buying in bulk. An easy solution is to build an Excel spreadsheet that nets the cost of obsolescence and other factors. The EOQ can then be evaluated by the ordering quantity which gives the lowest cost. The mathematical formulation provides a quicker way of evaluating EOQ but with limitation as you can see, but with the power of computing we can easily achieve the same outcome which would have taken a longer time in the past.

Here's a spreadsheet example that has been built to include the cost of obsolescence and bulk discount.

Inputs	Description
Cost of material	The component pricing including discount for bulk purchase
Inventory Holding cost	Per annum cost of holding inventory, your finance team should be able to advise the annum cost of holding
Cost per order	Trucking cost etc. associated to each order. In some cases the cost is already factored into the cost of material
Annual Demand	Total annual demand (In this case the consumption is assumed consistent)
Shelf life	This goes into the cost of expiry calculation when buying in bigger lot size

Here's a partial sample of the table (Data to the right are not shown due to page space constraint). We are looking for the combination that gives the lowest annual net cost.

Order quantity	10,000	20,000	30,000	40,000	50,000
Inventory cost	$750	$1,500	$2,250	$3,000	$3,750
Cost of expiry	$ -	$ -	$ -	$ -	$ -
Cost of ordering	$5,000	$2,500	$1,667	$1,250	$1,000
Material cost	$250,000	$250,000	$250,000	$250,000	$250,000
Net cost	$255,750	$254,000	$ 253,917	$254,250	$254,750

And here's the result; you can see from the graph below that order quantity of 100,000 units will gives the best cost advantage for this scenario. For readers who are familiar with Linear programming or Excel Solver function, the same can be used to solve and locate the optimal EOQ.

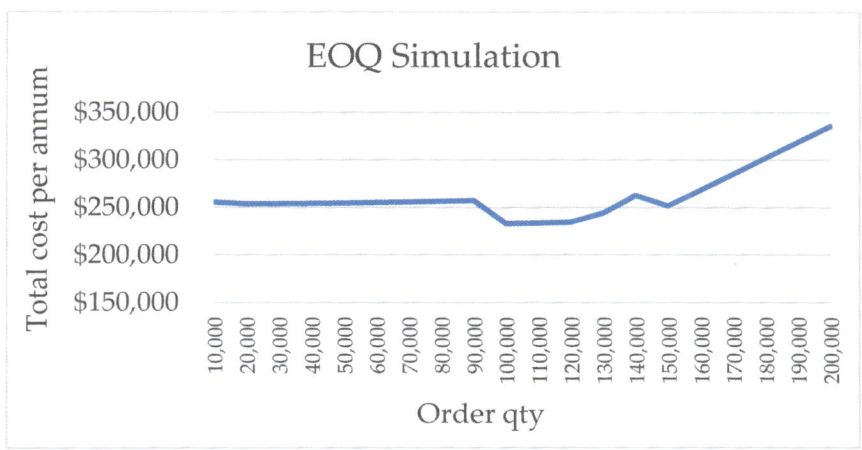

Another variant of ordering strategy is to pre-order in big quantity, but have it delivered later at more regular but in small batch sizes. Such arrangement benefits the supplier as well, as the volumes are committed upfront. It is not pragmatic to use a single formula to optimize the supply chain since there are several permutations of purchase behavior.

Data analytics is all about being able to understand the fundamental business processes with a good comprehension of using the rights analytical tools and building simulation models to bring new insights and create new solutions with the changing environment.

Manufacturing case study

In this section, we are going to discuss a specific case study of some high volume electronic manufacturing line, and demonstrating how data analytic can add value.

A project team was assembled to study opportunities in improving the production line capacity. The production line was highly automated; it was running several processes linked by conveyers. Some steps were running batch processing, while some were single part process. At some pre-defined stages in the manufacturing, parts were sampled for online or offline testing. The team wanted to know which process they could work on to improve the capacity needed to meet future growth in demand requirements.

As a start, data was gathered on the tool run rate, yield and downtime. Here's the table that was put together.

	Machine #1	Machine #2	Machine #3	Machine #4
Parts per min	53	49	52	50
Individual Yield	95%	100%	95%	98%
Downtime	20%	15%	25%	20%
Daily Capability	58,003	59,976	53,352	56,448
Cum Yield	88%	93%	93%	98%
Target capability	57,098	54,243	54,243	51,531
Target output	**50,500**			

Using the Parts per minute, yield and subtracting downtime, the daily capacity for each machine was calculated. With a daily target line output of 50,500, the team worked backwards to determine the individual target capacity required at each machines. This was done considering cumulative yield effect, meaning the first machine will have to produce more factoring the yield loses as it goes downstream. The target capacity for Machine#1 was 57,098 and its daily capacity was 58,003, so this machine met the output requirement and did not require improvement action. Through this exercise, only machine 3 was identified as not being able to meet the targeted capacity. This was a standard capacity analysis approach used by engineering team all along, but did you spot the problem? Let me explain.

When machines are linked in a chain manners using conveyer, they are tightly coupled. The conveyer space between the two processes is the only "buffer" space that absorbs any inefficiency or downtime between the processes. A tightly coupled environment has the following characteristics:-

Downtime is cumulative - Downtime in one process will directly impact the next or previous process once the buffer in the conveyer gets used up or completely filled. The upstream machine stops building when the conveyer gets filled; similarly the next processes can only run until it runs out of parts on the conveyer. The length of the conveyer is crucial if one of the process has frequent stoppages due to reasons like material change, intermittent error etc. An alternative is to include manual offloading of parts into a temporary storage to prevent the upstream process from stopping. Such manual intervention process could potentially add handling problems, and therefore fixing the root cause is still the best solution.

Bottleneck sets the pace - Imagine participating in a 5 legged 50m race. In the group you have a team member who can individually sprint 50m in 11 seconds, but then you also have a team member that covers the same distance in 25 seconds. Asking the team to run as fast as they could, you would have by now already guessed that the fastest the team could reach 50m mark will be 25 seconds.

Yield loss at bottleneck - Another illustration of the bottleneck concept can be seen in the figure below. Imagine a drainage system with a bottleneck. Regardless of how big the drain is scaled upstream or downstream, the water can only flow as fast as what the bottleneck is. In fact water will be blocked and accumulated before bottleneck, while water that comes right after the bottlenecks is flushed out immediately. Imagine running your machines in a similar manner; you will see parts accumulated before the bottleneck (This is actually one quick way to see where your bottleneck is). Yield losses at bottleneck will cause further deterioration in the downstream capacity.

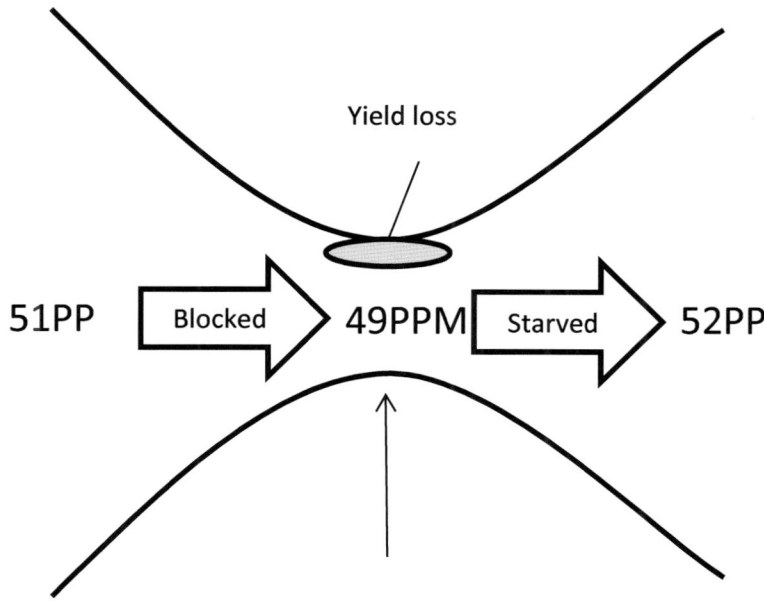

Sometimes the manufacturing machines are modular, and so they are loosely coupled. Since the processes are separated, it creates the convenience of buffering which allows the downtime between machines to be decoupled. This is a possible solution if the processes or machines are fairly unstable with a lot of intermittent stoppages. However, loosely coupled processes also means potential inventory challenge since buffers are kept everywhere.

Now let's go back to the capacity table tabulated earlier. The scenario discussed is a tightly coupled process. In the earlier calculation it was shown that only Machine #3 was not meeting the target capacity of 54,243. Let's re-examine the result before we show it to the head of engineering department.

At steady state (not considering downtime), all machines can only run at the pace set by the bottleneck. Therefore the run rate for each machine is limited to 49 parts per minute. Since the bottleneck (Machine #2) has 100% yield we do not need to consider the effect of yield loses. What about the downtime? It is almost impossible to calculate the downtime due to the chain effects of tightly coupled environment. One way to overcome this is to capture all non-production time as downtime. This includes tool idling time due to upstream downtime and tool waiting for downstream conveyer to be cleared of parts. Let's assume the downtime given in the table is already showing the total downtime. Now let's look at the new capacity table; considering the pace is determined by bottleneck PPM (Parts per minute).

	Machine #1	Machine #2	Machine #3	Machine #4
Parts per min	49	49	49	49
Individual Yield	95%	100%	95%	98%
Downtime	20%	15%	25%	20%
Daily Capability	53,626	59,976	50,274	55,319
Cum Yield	88%	93%	93%	98%
Target capability	57,098	54,243	54,243	51,531
Target Output	50,500			

At steady state run rate, the new intelligence has shown that more investment is required to address the bigger gap in Machine #3. Being constraint by the bottleneck, Machine #1 is also not able to produce the parts at the rate it is

supposed to. In order to address the capacity gap, you can follow this set of guidelines:-
- Improving the yield before bottleneck will not get you more output; it will however save you some cost from scrappage. To get more output, yield improvements has to be done at bottleneck or after
- Only run rate improvements at bottleneck will help in more output, and the next bottleneck after solving the first
- Focus resource on bottleneck, to prevent and reduce downtime e.g. SMED (Single-Minute Exchange of Die)
- Do not cause bottleneck to stop due to no incoming parts (Starving) or outgoing conveyer full (Blocked)
- As you improve the bottleneck situation, the bottleneck might shift and you then apply the same guideline again

Off-the-shelf various commercial simulation tools are available to model and prove the similar theory as explained above. However it's a reality that simulation knowledge is usually scarce and takes a sizeable amount of time to prepare, build and test a model. Simulation offers detailed study and quantification of ROI for different scenarios. As you can see from the above example, we were able to mine the information and identified key area for improvements. Hence, be creative with what can be achieved through careful analysis of data.

Channel order case study

We were asked by ABC Company to investigate the reasons behind the periodical order spikes, causing stock out leading to air shipment expedites. Symptoms were showing order spikes taking place almost every 3 months; such spikes would cause stock availability issues and air freights were the answer to help with recovery.

Here's a simplified view of the supply chain.

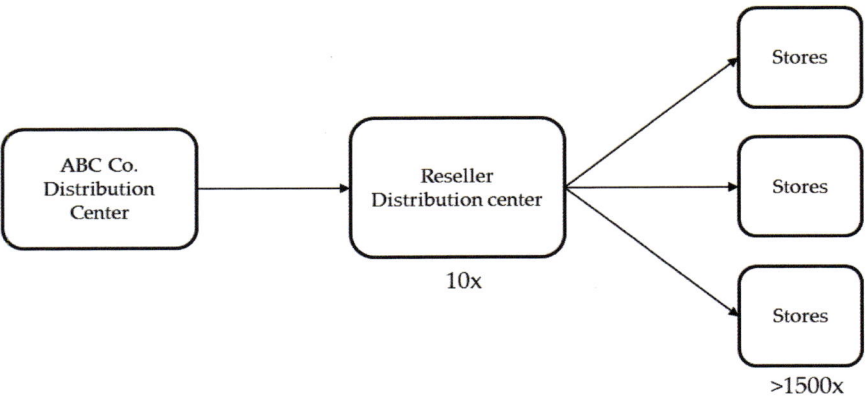

The regional distribution center takes orders from resellers on daily basis. Orders were then shipped to the reseller distribution center for further distribution to their stores; in this case there were more than 1500 stores managed by single reseller. How the reseller was deciding on the order quantity requirements was unknown at the beginning of the study. We felt this was the critical information needed to get to the root of the issue.

Retailer replenishment behavior

We started by first understanding buying behavior of customers at the stores. The chart below shows the daily order from retailer (Line chart) versus the quantity sold to customer (Area chart) by that reseller over a period of time. It can be seen clearly that customers buying pattern were very much linear, but orders placed back to ABC were following erratic pattern. In fact order variation shows a 2x to 4x magnification as it goes through the reseller replenishment process.

Quarter end push

Here's a further zoom in details showing the Retailer inventory versus the spikey Retailer orders versus Customer demand all in a single chart. The inventory will be a function of what was carried over from the last period, minus customer demand, plus what the retailer had ordered and received from ABC.

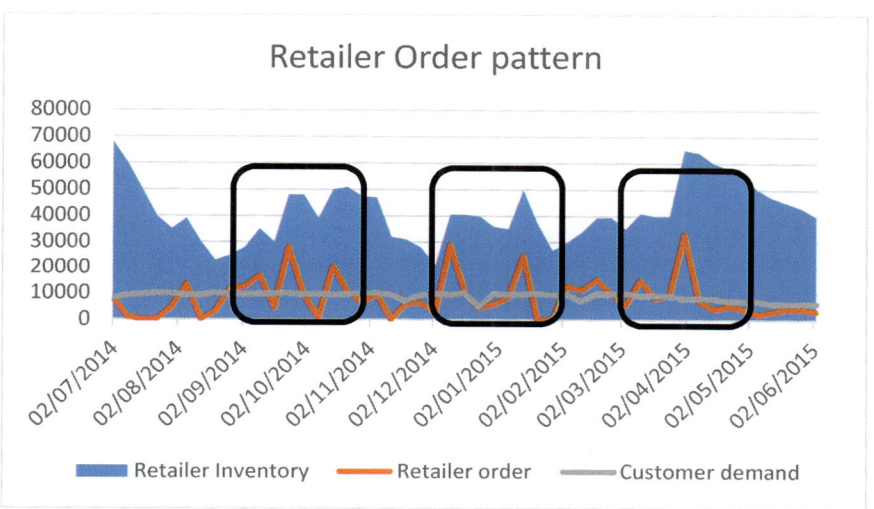

Let's take a look at the periods marked out by the 3 rectangles. Orders from retailer were showing spikey behavior despite customer's purchase being very stable. We also noticed that the spikey orders were above customer's average purchase (Approximately 10,000 units). Retailer inventory level started to increase indicating a stocking behavior rather than demand driven by customers' purchases. Once stock level shoots up, what happened next? In order to deplete the higher inventory, retailer cuts their orders to ABC soon after (dip in retailer orders immediately following the spike). We wanted to understand what was driving this peculiar behavior.

The period marked were actually the quarter end months. ABC Company in order to meet the quarterly revenue target would run promotions to increase sales towards quarter end closing. This helped to increase sales figure at quarter end, but sales for following month was again low, since retailer had to first clear their stock from the big orders placed at the recent quarter end. This became a vicious cycle where orders on month 1 of the quarter were softer, and promotions and price discounts tactics had to be offered to meet quarterly sales in month 3. This seasonality created other problems for the supply chain, such as:-

- High demand in month 3 required higher capacity sizing throughout the whole supply chain
- Air shipments had to be used to re-stock due to the artificial demand; problem propagated upstream to factory raw material supply as well
- The spikey behavior instituted fear of stock-out, thus each supply chain nodes started to keep more buffer

You can see how much cost and inventory ABC Company was incurring to maintain this vicious cycle. The issue of poorly managing quarter end promotions and price discounts as a way to meet the sales figures is commonly witnessed across many companies.

Low volume versus high volume behavior

The graph below shows the order variation in different products with different volume of demand, starting with low volume on the left towards high volume on the right. As mentioned earlier customer order variation were typically lower, and through retailers replenishment process the variation got magnified 2 to 4 times.

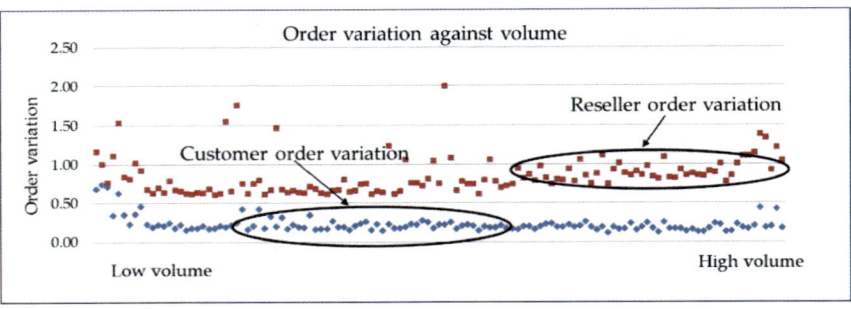

On the left we can see that order variation from customers were higher for lower volume SKUs. Consumption for low volume products typically exhibits a more erratic behavior due to smaller pool of users. What is interesting is that the order magnification (retailer order variation/ customer order variation) for low volume parts were lower as compared to high volume products. This was mainly due to the smaller MOQ (minimum order quantity) and packing size. For higher volume orders the MOQ were higher, and when several orders were placed together, it created a bigger spikes. Therefore, order magnifications was higher compared to lower volume products.

A strange behavior was observed with the highest volume grouping on the extreme right. The magnification factor was highest, but why? Was it due to higher MOQ requirements? Initial observation showed that the placed orders were much higher than MOQ, and they were for a pallet size quantity (MOQ was much lower than a pallet quantity). To reduce handling cost, ABC Company had an agreement with reseller that offered them a discount for placing orders for full pallet quantities. This helped ABC reduce handling costs by not being involved in breaking up the package from pallets. However, they didn't foresee the resulting consequences that came with order spike. ABC Company's distribution center and the upstream supply chain had to scramble to replenish the orders. This was purely the result of silo optimization.

These insights were enlightening to the management team. There were some aspects in the findings they could change easily; others needed some time before people could adapt them and achieve cost efficiencies. Quarter end acceleration may not go away, but with better forecasting in place company can anticipate demand fluctuations and minimize last minute rush through the supply chain.

CHAPTER 6

INVENTORY MANAGEMENT DATA ANALYSIS

"The Myth and Science…"

Investors look at the state of company's inventory to gauge its operational efficiency & cash flow status. High inventory not only reflect tied up cash but also means high warehousing cost as well. Further the rapidly changing trends in technology advancements possess depreciation and obsolescence risk in holding high inventory. We shall discuss the topic of analyzing inventory and safety stock data in good detail since this is an important topic for supply chain.

Days of Inventory
Inventories are commonly measured by two metrics:-
- Days of Inventory
- Annual Inventory turn

Days of Inventory (DOI)
The formula for calculating DOI is as follow:-

$$DOI = (365 * Avg\ Inventory) / (Annual\ COGS)$$

Annual Inventory Turns
Another form of expressing inventory is Inventory turns.

$$Inventory\ Turns = \frac{365}{DOI} \quad OR \quad Inventory\ Turns = \frac{Annual\ COGS}{Avg\ Inventory}$$

DOI or Inventory Turns varies widely across different industries and different supply chain models. To stay competitive, companies are always looking for means to reduce their inventory and increase inventory turns. Below are some inventory optimization strategies that can be executed:-

- Purchase semi-finished goods where possible than manufacturing in-house(cutting supply chain length)
- Supply chain network re-design
- Reduce replenishment lead-time (sourcing supplier closer to you)
- More frequent planning
- Review the EOQ, order frequency, batch size of processes
- Improve forecast accuracy
- Execute late product postponement strategy
- Ship air (short product life cycle which depreciates fast with new technology e.g. Computer)
- Move BTS (Build to stock) to BTO (Build to Order) environment
- Rationalize product proliferation
- Improve manufacturing Lead-time (less WIP, faster response thus

lesser safety stock)
- Optimize inventory strategy within the company (Safety stock setting)

Although inventory optimization is important for cash flow, however reduction of inventory must be carefully executed with consideration to service level and cost associated with expediting shipments to protect availability. It is crucial to learn the various data analysis processes available in reducing inventory, without compromising the other supply chain metrics.

There are 3 categories of inventory:-
- Work In Progress (WIP) / Transit
- Cycle stock
- Safety stock

In some discussion you might have heard about Structured versus Strategic inventory. It is a different way of inventory classification but essentially is the same concept. Structured inventory is inventory arise as a result of structural processes such as transit and batching. It is very much determined by the process structure itself. Driving structural inventory down will require redesigning the process flow e.g. Network redesign or looking for a faster way to complete a process. Strategic inventory is pure Safety Stock, it exist only for one reason; "protection". Here's a pictorial representation of the various types of inventories. Cycle stock is present wherever process flow size are in batch size bigger than 1.

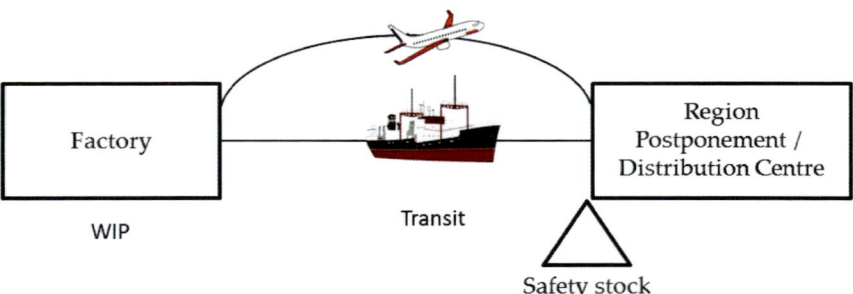

To understand how to optimize the inventory we will start by discussing each component and show how you can tackle them individually.

WIP / Transit
Little's Law states, the average number of customers in a stable system is equal to the rate of customer arrival multiply by the time they spend in the

system.

Inventory in WIP is modeled by Little's Law, in the same form:-

WIP = Mean Throughput x Cycle Time

Where:-

Throughput is the rate/ speed of the process
Cycle Time is the average time taken for the parts to travel from start to end of the process

For a manufacturing process, you will have to reduce the time taken for the parts to flow through the system. Value stream mapping technique can be used to map the process and material flow. Reducing the non-value add process will help optimize the cycle time and therefore reduce the WIP inventory.

Transit inventory is usually the biggest bucket of inventory for a supply chain. In today's global supply chain environment, it is very common to outsource or have manufacturing sites across the globe. Now as the supply chains become more stratified, inventory due to transportation of goods becomes higher. Raw material and semi-finished goods has to be transported from one geographical site to another. Here are some possible approaches to help alleviate the impact:-

- Ship using Air (not the best tradeoff but possible in some cases due to high value of goods and inventory holding cost)
- Mixed mode (hybrid between ocean and land transport, might cost more than ocean route but offers tradeoff for shorter transit time)
- Depending on the contractual agreement, raw material can be purchased and own by the contract manufacturer (Turnkey arrangement)

Safety stock
Safety stocks are used everywhere in supply chain to buffer against forecast error and inefficiencies. When set correctly it can be used for trading off against higher factory upside requirements and air shipments (as discussed earlier). However in most part safety stock is used to mask and protect against inefficiencies in the supply chain. Most of the buyers we interviewed lacked proficiencies around establishing appropriate buffer sizes and we found high levels of safety stock were the result of iterative adjustment made every time a stock-out was encountered. Most organizations lack the diligence or

capabilities to analyze the root cause for the shortage and fear becomes the driving mechanism behind high safety stock settings.

Safety stock setting should be statistical and not an emotional driven process. Inventory problems should be analyze and fixed. Simply adding new buffer is not the appropriate way to deal with the problem situation. In the following sections we will share few case studies on how safety stock setting process can help enable a higher customer satisfaction experience. Let's begin by understanding the formula for safety stock setting.

Safety Stock (units) $= k * \sqrt{\mu^2 * S^2 + (L + R) * \sigma^2}$ or

Safety Stock (Days) $= k * \sqrt{S^2 + (L + R) * COV^2}$

Where:-

k = Service level constant
μ = Average forecasted demand
S = Supplier Lead-time variation
L+R = Replenishment Lead-time
σ = Standard Deviation Forecast error
COV = Coefficient of variance

The formula assumes forecast error is random and can be represented by a normal distribution curve with average forecast error being 0. In most cases forecast errors are not zero (biased), and should be corrected at the forecast and not through adjustment of safety stock.

The variable k represents the Z values from a list of confidence interval required by the customer. Higher the service level, the higher is the value of Z, which can be looked up from the Z/ Normal table.

There are 3 key components in the square root function: - Supply variation, Lead-time and Forecast error.

Supply Variation
S and μ both represents the required protection against supplier variability. S represents the standard deviation for supplier delay against targeted lead-time. Multiplying Supplier variability with Average forecasted demand (μ) gives you the level of stock required to cover against the potential delays.

Lead-Time

The second part of the safety stock equation includes protection for forecast error for a given lead-time. The quantity of safety stock needed to protect against forecast error is fundamentally determined by the additional demand units consumed before new replenishment stock can arrive (Lead-time). There are two components in Lead-time:- Review frequency and order lead-time. Review frequency refers to the frequency or the interval at which stock levels are being monitored. Order lead-time represents the total time from the moment orders are placed to the time order are received. Adding the two components together represents the total response time required from stock monitoring to stock receipt.

Setting supplier lead time can sometimes be confusing. There could be a situation wherein supplier takes 3 months to manufacture the parts, and another 2 months to deliver. So would you use 5 months as lead-time? It depends on if the supplier is provided with the forecast or not. If supplier is getting a forecast then it should be able to prepare the raw material and probably pre-build the components. In this situation the order lead-time should be measured against how fast the ordered components can be delivered from their stocking point and not from the raw state.

COV (Coefficient of variance)/ Forecast error

The standard deviation for a high volume runner product is much higher than a lower volume product. It is unrealistic to compare the forecast error variation directly to conclude if one is better than the other, since the volumes are different. COV is calculated simply by taking the forecast error standard deviation and dividing it by the average daily forecast. This produce a ratio of forecast error variation to the volume. We can now compare COV between products to determine if one is better than the other. As you may see in the second safety stock formula, COV can be used directly to calculate safety stock in days of supply as well as. COV information is very helpful. If your product has a high COV or high forecast error then you should be working on to reducing the product lead time. This could mean, working with suppliers to position the safety stock closer to you, creating strategically placed inventory buffers to reduce the lead time and etc. If you have a low COV or low forecast error, work on eliminating the variability in the supply of the product. This could mean focusing on processes, getting more reliable and higher quality suppliers etc.

Dead stock

We realized that it is always a challenge when it comes to safety stock setting, discussion with stakeholders are difficult as emotion tends to drive a lot of push back in lowering buffer targets. Building confidence and changing culture takes times.

We were once requested to create an analytics driven visual indicator to help assist people to make a better judgment, setting the stage for data driven decision making. Quantifying Dead-stock information is actually quite a straight forward process. Dead-stock is a measure of "un-used" stock. If you monitor stock level at a particular storage location the minimum level of stock across a period of time is call Dead-stock. What this essentially means is that since inventory level does no go below this Dead-stock level, you are actually over stocking. Dead-stock information is gathered first by plotting the daily inventory trend at a certain location. The inventory trend will show the periods of peaks and valley over the period of study. If you notice that inventory does reach a stock-out situation, you may want to adjust the safety stock. However, if the inventory always stays at healthy level that is an indicator that safety stock levels might be set too high.

Refer to the below inventory trend for product A. Inventory trend showed presence of a high level of Deadstock. According to the buyer, the production manager had asked for a safety stock setting that that would avoid stock out in all situations. The target was chosen and since there wasn't an issue, no one felt the need to review the target anymore. This is a common behavior that stem from fear that drives the decision making. However with this data analysis, no one could argue and disagree with what the data was depicting. The buffer cut was made and inventory was reduced.

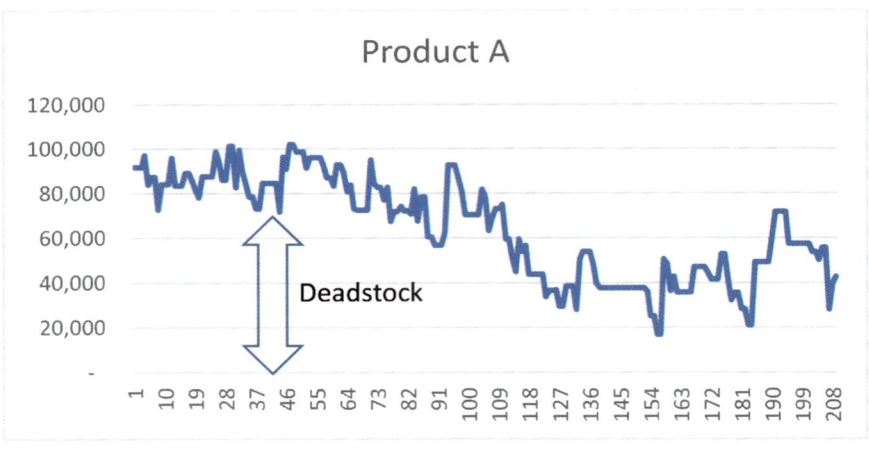

Here's an example for another Product B.

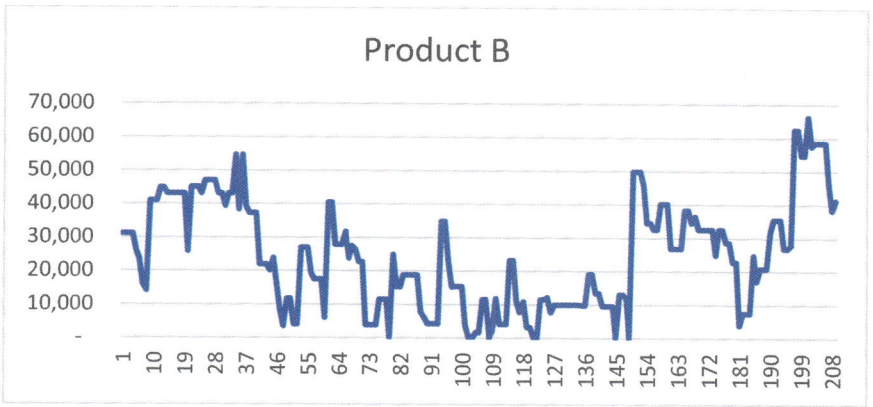

In this case we can see the inventory for Product B is operating at a low level, and occasionally hitting stock out. This requires a review to determine if the stock out levels were according to customer service level requirements and accordingly safety stock settings needs to be adjusted.

When it comes to safety stock calculation and proposal, Deadstock charting is a powerful tool to convince the business stakeholders that a change in safety stock is necessary. In our experience we have found this a lot easier for stakeholders to accept than a result from a pure statistic. Analysis like these helps accelerate the building of confidence for an analytics environment.

Safety stock poor practices

Safety stock is considered the easiest knob to use when it comes to inventory reduction pressures. In this section, we are going to showcase examples of usual safety stock mismanagement processes.

Here are some of the common safety stock control techniques being used, and we shall discuss each in more details.

- Butter spread approach
- Wrong use of ABC technique
- Quarter end inventory clamp down

Butter Spread approach
Safety stock calculation requires the support of data availability. However, in most cases, data is not readily available, and collecting data is a daunting task. Moreover people usually do not have the bandwidth or the capacity to perform calculation for hundreds or thousands of parts. In such cases, the

easiest solution is to apply a common safety stock setting to group of components. Seems like a familiar situation?

Let's look at some real data to understand the issue with this approach. We carried out a study for a group of components over different demand volume.

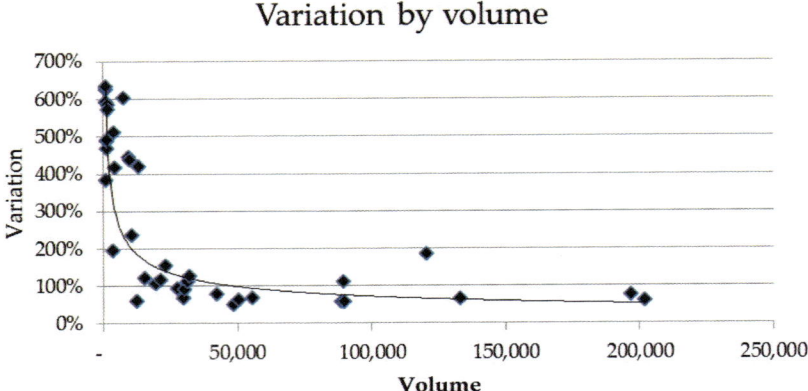

What is interesting, however not surprising is that order variation differs across products. You can see that the lower demand volume products tend to be more volatile. So if you execute a butter spread safety stock target setting approach, you will either end up with a huge over-protection or a frequent stock-out situation. Either case it is going to cost your company dearly.

ABC Approach

ABC method is a popular inventory categorization technique that allows different levels of attention being put against different categories of goods. "A" category products are those that are considered important either due to the high product cost or the high indirect cost e.g. sales values. Products in group A requires more frequent monitoring than those in group B and C. Products in C grouping are those that you wish to pay the least attention to, or has minimal impact to the organization even if it is not monitored closely. The key benefit with such clustering is that the organization scarce resources can be guided to focus on products with higher returns.

When we were first invited to perform a thorough safety stock analysis with this particular Company, we were told that the purchasing department was religiously using ABC technique to manage its finished goods inventory. As such, products grouped in A and B had their safety stock reviewed on a quarterly basis, while safety stock review for products in C grouping were not performed due to low volume nature.

The business was under tight inventory budget and couldn't afford to increase their inventory size to reduce the current stock-out instances. Customers were of course not happy and the CEO was getting direct escalations from the big account customers seeking solution for the problem.

We started by gathering the Forecast error history data by product level. Through calculations and review of the new safety stock numbers we made following observations:-

- The highest runners have safety stock setting well above the calculated safety stock recommendations, and they were not stocking out
- Certain group C products have safety stock set too low for the amount of forecast error seen, and there were more backlog instances

It turns out that although there was a process for safety stock calculation and review, account managers were manually overriding the recommended values based on the fact that group A products were crucial to the company's overall revenue. Fear overtook statistics, and safety stock for group A's product were thus set higher to protect availability. Inventory budget was then offset by setting the rest of the products with a lower safety stock target. Nobody paid attention to group C products, as it was not supposed to be important. ABC approach was obviously abused and misinterpreted for fear. Excess inventory situation was resulted solely driven by the need to create that extra protection (which was not even due to availability issue) on the high product volume runners than the lower ones. The company was getting escalations from the customers mainly due to B and C parts, as they were running with lean buffers and tighter budget was hampering the elevation of safety stock settings. Those budget could have easily be funded from fraction of budget that was allocated to unnecessarily increase in the A product safety stock levels.

Analytics process is incomplete until solution is proposed and implemented. The team implemented the proposal of setting up a quarterly governance process. The new process enforced tight governance in setting safety stock, and analytics is used as a basis for safety stock target decision making. The safety stock for all products were reviewed, and more liberal targets were set for C products to avoid frequent escalations merely due to a small volume misses.

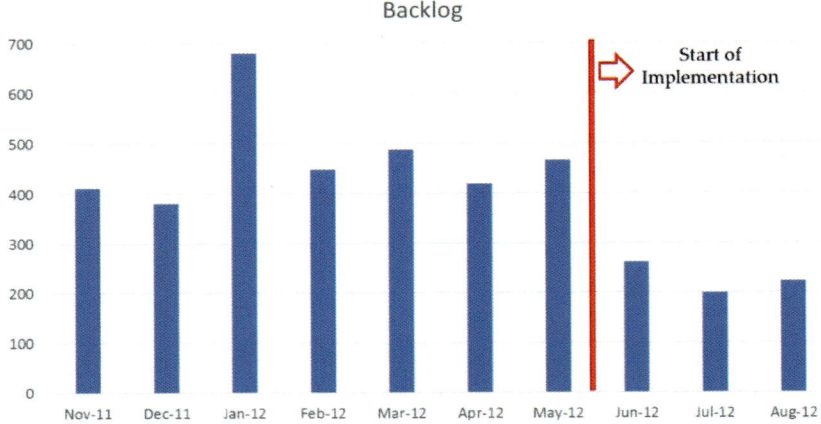

Chart above shows the numbers of backlog misses post implementation of the new governance process. We can see clearly that the backlog count was reduced by half and sustained during the period of monitoring. The result was achieved with merely rebalancing the safety stock allocation and adopting data analytics as a framework for setting the right protection level.

Quarter end Clamp
One very common phenomenon we have seen is how inventories are being controlled at the quarter end. Companies reports their quarter end inventory holding, and while inventory may be high other times, it somehow must be clamped down during quarter end. Guess what, safety stock is the easiest knob to accomplish that. Supply chain usually resort to cutting safety stock levels during quarter end to meet their budget. Can you think of some risks associated with the approach?

As sales team are trying aggressively to meet their quarterly targets by pushing sales, the supply chain teams are trying on the other hand to manage the inventory and setting a lower target. This behavior of lowering safety stock is just a perfect storm waiting for customer escalation. This results in panic, confusion, late night conferences and costly air shipments to answer demand.

Cutting safety stock at the quarter end has an impact to manufacturing too. Manufacturing capacity is fixed by the resources, both in steel (machines) and labor. Manufacturing favors linear loaded volume and there is a capacity limits to how much additional volume it can build within a certain time frame. Lowering safety stock at end quarter means that factories have to slow down the build. At the start of the new quarter, safety stock gets reset to the original level; now factory has to catch up with the demand it dropped during the earlier quarter end. This is only achievable if factory has that volume of extra capacity. To recover to original safety stock level takes time and this may very well means air shipment may be needed to aid in speed of recovery. We have seen this behavior numerous times going through data showing higher air shipments post quarter end.

Poor inventory management is the biggest cause for unhappy customers, besides burdening the company's operating cost and impacting the bottom line. The good news is that through proper data understanding and management, we can essentially overcome the issue and bring significant improvements to the business bottom line. We are going to share more real success stories and solutions.

BTO (Build to Order)

Order fulfilment strategy largely influences the replenishment cost and the inventory position for the company. Customer satisfaction is the number 1 priority in product deliveries, and so supply chain nodes are added closer to customer to gain efficiency in response time to the changing demands. Executing order fulfillment strategy efficiently gets challenged as product proliferation gets increased over time. Product differentiation are created to cater for needs of those customers looking for different values in the product. In some cases, creating regional product differentiation is necessary to help protect price point by deterring retailers who may otherwise exploit parallel import as a profit gaining mechanism. Also in certain cases to compete against competitors, regional teams or resellers may want to run a promotion event selling combo deals that requires new packaging options. These all are swelling the challenge of getting the right product build on time for the right distribution point.

Supply chain product distribution strategy favors keeping product at centralized location further upstream. Pooling of inventory has its advantage in reducing the impact due to forecast errors and complexity of supply chain distribution. Drawing from our experience we suggest bringing supply chain distribution closer to customers, but delaying our postponement of product to mitigate forecast inaccuracy. This is where supply chain optimization software fits in well. The software algorithm compares the customer order lead-time against replenishment lead times, and calculates the level of inventory requires at each of the nodes to ensure stocks are sufficient to cover effect of forecast error at each nodes. We will be replicating the same logic but using Excel, more on that to follow later.

We divide order fulfilment into two main categories; Build to order (BTO) and Build to forecast (BTF). Building to order means products are only created or build after the sales order is placed by customers. Predominantly, supply chain which operates in such manners involves large permutation of configuration or customization. Pre-configuring such products can means large amount of inventory waiting for orders, and potential obsolescence cost if orders does not materialize. Lead time for order fulfilment is critical in BTO. Therefore, the BTO supply chain must be sufficiently responsive such that it does not exceeds the time a customer is willing to wait for the product completion. Dell-direct model was once famous to envy of its competitor in executing this strategy flawlessly, as their customers was able to choose their PC's configuration and had it delivered in short period.

When customer places an order, they expect a quick product delivery turnaround. If the customer expected turnaround time is longer than what a supply chain is capable in delivering; BTO is the perfect model. If the supply chain response time is longer than what customer is expecting, stock has to be prebuild to ensure order can be fulfilled. In this case prebuild quantities are dependent on the forecast, and thus the strategy is to build to forecast. Inventories are needed whenever there is a mismatch in replenishment turnaround time requirement. The longer a customer acceptance to wait is, the further you can delay your product postponement and carry inventory pool upstream in the supply chain.

We were working on a project to evaluate inventory optimization and improved service level opportunity at a distribution center. Customer had high expectations for the delivery times. Products ordered had to be delivered to customers' warehouse within 5 days from order placement. On the supply chain end, order processing typically took 1 day and product postponement 2 days. Shipment preparation including product delivery to customer took from 1 to 4 days. Below is the diagram to illustrate the different timings.

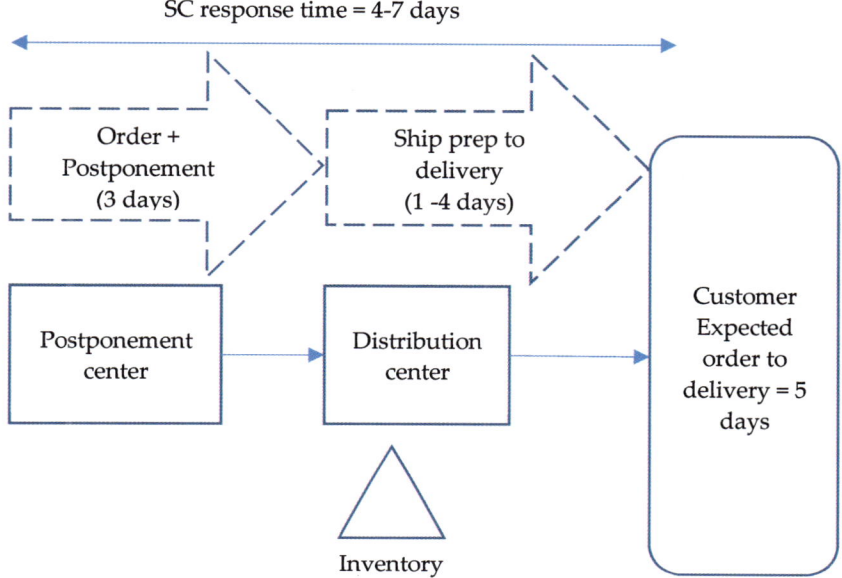

In this case supply chain response time was longer than the customer expected order to delivery time. They had no choice but to pre-build stock using the forecast. Finished goods inventory were placed in the distribution center in anticipation of customer orders. By placing enough inventories at the distribution center, the supply chain response time now fall in the range of 1 to 4 days, meeting customer expectations. The impact of BTF (Build to Forecast) in such cases is with the risk associated with the cost of carrying unused inventory due to forecast errors, and having to deal with product availability issues resulting from stocking wrong product mix or packing product in different packaging. This is a common problem faced from time to time in most supply chains.

What opportunities still lies beneath such constrained situation? We cannot execute BTO strategy since customers are expecting a faster turnaround than what the supply chain can deliver. You will be pleasantly surprised when we tell you that this is not entirely true and there is still an opportunity to meet customer response expectations following BTO strategy. If you re-study the supply chain map again, the customer is 1 day away from the distribution center. That gives us 4 days margin, which is more than sufficient for product postponement. The dates products must leave distribution center are worked backward from when products are required to be delivered, minus the transit time to ship the parts to customer.

Ship date = Required Delivery date - Delivery time

If Ship date is more than or equal to 3 days from order date that order qualifies for BTO. Inventory will only be built for orders which cannot wait for the 3 days turnaround. Converting qualified products to BTO mode helps to reduce the inventory holding at the distribution center, and since we perform product build upon getting orders, this helps to improves service level which otherwise suffer due to forecast errors.

Next question; how do you decide on the amount of stocking inventory required for product orders that do not qualified for BTO? Here's the concept:-

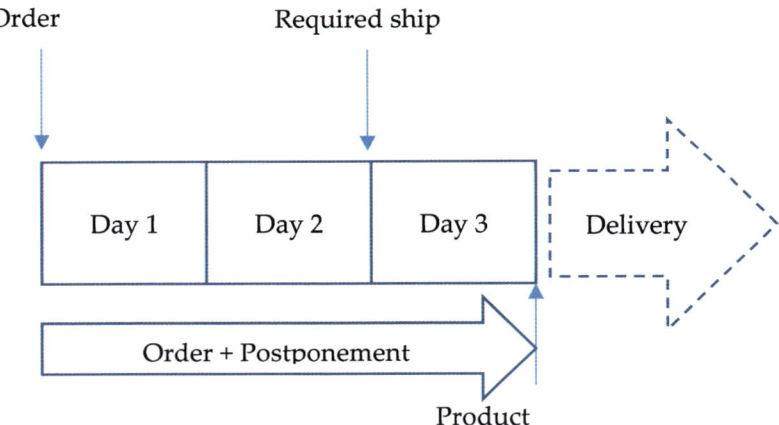

Upon receiving orders from the customers, it takes 3 days for the product to be packaged in the right configuration. For a product whose ship date is more than or equal 3 days from order placement, we can build it to order. The safety stock in the distribution center should only be catered to protecting orders that required ship dates that fall inside day 1 and day 2. Taking historical order data, we started screening out those orders that could have been BTO candidates. For the remaining data, we then started to sort them by the required ship date. This data represented the order quantity that needed to be shipped every day. We know that order postponement requires 3 days; so ideally there need to be 3 days' worth of inventory on any given day, before replenishment could arrive.

The order data we used for calculation went back more than 3 months; this was to make sure it included any form of orders irregularities and quarterly seasonality. Using Excel spreadsheet, we created a pivot table to show the order quantity by ship date. Row 3 is the moving sum of 3 days' worth of shipments for those non-BTO orders; this represent the replenishment lead-time required for postponement.

	A	B	C	D	E	F	G	H
1	Ship date	1/1/2016	1/2/2016	1/3/2016	1/4/2016	1/5/2016	1/6/2016	1/7/2016
2	Quantity	1000	2000	500	800	1200	300	2000
3	3 days inventory	=SUM(B2:D2)	3300	2500	2300	3500	2300	2000

Using data from row 3, we now calculates the inventory against desired service level using the Percentile function in Excel. Below is an illustration of how the formula looks like; in this case the data is in cell B3 to H3.

	A	B	C	D	E	F	G	H
1	Ship date	1/1/2016	1/2/2016	1/3/2016	1/4/2016	1/5/2016	1/6/2016	1/7/2016
2	Quantity	1000	2000	500	800	1200	300	2000
3	3 days inventory	3500	3300	2500	2300	3500	2300	2000
4								
5	95 Percentile	=percentile((B3:H3,95%)						

The implementation was highly successfully; there was a better precision now to rely on actual orders than using forecast previously. As a result, millions worth of inventories was taken off the system and availability to customer was improved as the impact of product mix issue was greatly reduced by delaying the postponement.

FINAL WORDS

Business leaders are more and more making decisions based on analytical insights driven by data. Hence, the dependency on data has grown more than before. Technological advances are helping companies to find and process information from new data points. Since speed at which the data is coming has enormously grown in magnitude, it requires new ways to capture and a new breed of human resource to deal with. Besides resources, the need for developing an analytics culture and capabilities is important more than before.

Undoubtedly, Supply chain of today faces enormous challenges as the global economy is becoming extremely dynamic and always transforming. The development of technology and enhanced tool capabilities has allowed analytics to not only expand and view system as a whole, but also aid in the speed of completing complex analysis in shorter time frames. It is important to capitalize on this advantage, and allow the company to stay ahead of its competitors.

Research has shown analytics is helping companies improve their market share. Furthermore, it makes companies more efficient and smarter. A smart organization operates more efficiently with a leaner workforce. Employees are more involved in performing value added activities than managing escalations. However, it does take time and investment to develop an analytics environment. Changing organization mindset and culture may take time, but this is the journey worth taking. If you or your organization has not started analytics, this is the time.

ABOUT THE AUTHOR

Samuel New is a certified 6 Sigma Black Belt and Lean Sigma professional. He has worked in various spectrums of Supply Chain for over 20 years. He has been leading multi-million dollar data analytics projects partnering across the globe to innovate solutions for inventory, cost, and availability. Sam is also an analytics mentor for his supply chain department, and is currently leading his various supply chain teams through an analytics transformation.

Rajesh Agnihotri has over 20 years of supply chain management experience. Over the years, he has helped companies formulate and implement supply chain solutions on a multitude of levels; from companies starting from scratch, to multibillion dollar global enterprises. He has utilized a broad range of data analytics techniques and tools to guide his business decisions. This has provided him with a great insight and visibility into the data analytics process. Rajesh holds an Executive MBA and Master's Degree in Engineering.